Praise for *Awesomely Simple*

John Spence understands business. Lucky for us, he wants
share his passion for success. *Awesomely Simple* is honest,
cere, and written with a commitment to discovering how
iness can work more effectively, productively, and profit-
y. We all get caught up in things that don't matter. John
ars the clutter, and then wonderfully illustrates what is
ly important to build success in business."
—**Joel Zeff,** national speaker and author, *Make the Right
Choice*

"Uncertain times require us to reconnect with the fundamentals. John Spence knows these fundamentals as well as
anyone, and his direct and simple style—supported with real-
world examples and applications—makes it easy for anyone
to understand and implement. There has never been a more
important time to revisit the themes in this great book."
—**Peter Sheahan,** author, *Flip* and *Generation Y*

"Are you looking for the keys to business success? John
Spence's new book helps you to find them! John truly makes
the very complex awesomely simple and shows you exactly
how to turn your ideas into a perfect winning strategy!"
—**Stefan Gubi,** president, AKG Acoustics, Vienna, Austria

"What we love about John is his ability to take the complex
business and financial services world we live in and make it
easy for all of us to understand. *Awesomely Simple* will help everyone make goal setting, strategy, and vision more focused
on relationships and people."
—**Randy Schleeter,** agency field executive, State Farm Insurance and Financial Services

AWESOMELY
SIMPLE

ESSENTIAL BUSINESS STRATEGIES

for

TURNING IDEAS INTO ACTION

JOHN SPENCE

JOSSEY-BASS
A Wiley Imprint
www.josseybass.com

Published by Jossey-Bass
A Wiley Imprint
One Montgomery, Ste. 1200, San Francisco, CA 94104—www.josseybass.com

Readers should be aware that Internet Web sites offered as citations and/or
sources for further information may have changed or disappeared between the
time this was written and when it is read.

Limit of Liability/Disclaimer of Warranty: While the publisher and author have
used their best efforts in preparing this book, they make no representations
or warranties with respect to the accuracy or completeness of the contents of
this book and specifically disclaim any implied warranties of merchantability
or fitness for a particular purpose. No warranty may be created or extended
by sales representatives or written sales materials. The advice and strategies
contained herein may not be suitable for your situation. You should consult with
a professional where appropriate. Neither the publisher nor author shall be liable
for any loss of profit or any other commercial damages, including but not limited
to special, incidental, consequential, or other damages.

Jossey-Bass books and products are available through most bookstores. To contact
Jossey-Bass directly call our Customer Care Department within the U.S. at 800-956-
7739, outside the U.S. at 317-572-3986, or fax 317-572-4002.

Jossey-Bass also publishes its books in a variety of electronic formats. Some
content that appears in print may not be available in electronic books.

Library of Congress Cataloging-in-Publication Data
Spence, John.
   Awesomely simple : essential business strategies for turning ideas into action /
John Spence.
       p.   cm.
   Includes index.
   ISBN 978-0-470-49451-6 (cloth)
     1. Success in business.   2. Business planning   3. Organizational
effectiveness.   4. Business enterprises.   I. Title.
   HF5386.S7514   2009
   658.4'012—dc22
                                                              2009018599

Printed in the United States of America
FIRST EDITION
HB Printing   10

To my amazing wife, Sheila. You are my best friend, my business partner, my life partner, my everything—forever.

CONTENTS

AWESOMELY
SIMPLE

Introduction

Iam totally addicted to business. I have had a two-business-books-a-week habit for nearly twenty years now. I can't help myself: I love studying business, I love running businesses, and I love working with employees and customers. To me, it is all a huge, fun, exciting game—a game, I might add, that if played well, can make you a lot of money. My greatest joy, though, comes from teaching businesspeople how to run their companies better. I realized a few years ago that most businesspeople are so busy working "in" their companies that they do not take any time to work "on" their companies. Frankly that scares me, because I know that if a businessperson is not taking serious time to study, learn, think, strategize, and innovate, pretty soon he or she will be forced to take some time to learn about something else: bankruptcy.

But in today's crazy-fast business world, who has time to read the top four hundred or five hundred business books and spend countless hours poring over thousands of pages of research findings to figure out what they all mean? How many business managers, directors, and owners have direct access to dozens of the top business leaders in America and can reach out to them for help and advice? How many businesspeople get the chance to crawl around in literally hundreds of other companies to watch what they do right and what they do wrong so they can apply those ideas in their own company? Well, I do.

For the past fifteen years, I have traveled around the world to work with every type of company from tiny mom-and-pops, tech start-ups, local governments, and nonprofits to global firms like Microsoft, Abbott Labs, State Farm, IBM, and GE. Most of these projects have been multiyear engagements in which I have had the opportunity to work shoulder-to-shoulder on critical projects with some of the best and worst businesspeople imaginable. I have spent years looking for the pattern of what differentiates great companies from great failures. What I have learned is that business is much less complex than I thought. Whether you have two people on the payroll or twenty-two thousand, the truth is that building a great company rests on just a few fundamental principles that are not complex or confusing in any way. Actually, as you'll soon find out, they are quite simple. My goal in writing this book, and in fact, one of the driving forces of my life, is to make the very complex awesomely simple. I want to give you the benefit of my twenty-plus years of high-level business experience in the pages that follow. My goal is to help you understand what it truly takes to build and sustain a successful company. And I will do this not just from my point of view, but from a synthesis of the best practices and key strategies of the leading companies in the world. We will look at numerous examples of how small and big companies, from high-tech to high-touch, climbed to the top of their industries. Everything you will read in this book is from real life: you'll find no fluff, no grand theories, no intellectual backflips. I want to make closing the gap between knowing something and actually doing it (what I refer to in this book as the knowing-doing gap) as easy as possible for you by giving you clear and straightforward advice about how to make any business run much, much better. As you'll see, it is not nearly as complicated as most people think it is. The real challenge, and the foundation for lasting business success, is the consistent and disciplined application of just six principles, day in and day out, in every part of your organization:

The Six Principles of Business Success

1. Vivid vision
2. Best people
3. Robust communication
4. Sense of urgency
5. Disciplined execution
6. Extreme customer focus

Every successful organization I have ever worked with, regardless of size, geography, or industry, understood that these six principles form the bedrock of their success and focused on them relentlessly. On the flip side, when I am called in to save a struggling company that stands on the brink of failure, it is usually because they are not doing one or more of these six key things effectively.

On the surface, these six principles may seem very simple, and for the most part they are. But "simple" in no way means "easy to implement." Tiger Woods makes playing golf look very simple, but there is nothing easy about what it took for him to get to that level of expertise. Recently I read *The Cambridge Handbook of Expertise and Expert Performance* in which the world's foremost "experts on expertise" reviewed all of the latest scientific research on how experts develop their superior skills. I won't drag you through all 901 pages of scientific findings. Basically what I felt the book said is that it takes four things to become an expert at anything—what I call the four P's:

■ ■ ■

- *Passion*. You have to love your area of focus. It needs to be an all-encompassing, driving force in your life if you ever hope to attain any level of real expertise in it.
- *Persistence*. According to the *Cambridge Handbook*, there is a phenomenon called "the ten-year rule." Nearly every expert studied had spent a minimum of seven to ten years (roughly 100,000 hours) working diligently at gaining skills and knowledge in an area of expertise. Even child prodigies like Mozart began their studies at a very early age, so by the time they reached adolescence, they had satisfied the ten-year rule. (Tiger started playing golf when he was only three.)
- *Practice*. During those seven to ten years, the experts consistently pushed themselves harder and harder, through more and more challenging practice sessions. This is what is referred to as "deliberate practice." Practice specifically focused toward working on weaknesses, getting feedback from coaches and expert mentors on strategies for improvement, making adjustments, and then practicing more and

more in a quest to achieve the highest possible proficiency in their area of expert performance.

- *Pattern recognition.* At the highest level, those who have crossed the threshold into true expertise have spent so much time focusing, practicing, and working on their area of passion that they begin to see patterns emerge. It is this pattern recognition that allows them to quickly decide the best course of action, the option that will yield optimal results. This is what is meant when a person talks about a chess grandmaster being able to "see down board." This is how great basketball players say they can "see the entire court." This is how Gretzky could skate to where the puck was going to be, not to where it was. This is how Tiger can visualize a hundred different ways to hit the ball from a difficult lie and consistently choose the winning shot. And this is how I have been able to see the patterns of success and failure in the hundreds of companies I've worked in.

■ ■ ■

In this book, I am not merely going to tell you what the pattern of successful companies is. I am going to tell you exactly how to apply these critical strategies in your organization and give you lots of examples and workshops to help make sure that you execute them effectively and consistently.

Why I Wrote This Book

I never had it as a major life goal to become an expert on business excellence. I was most concerned with finding a career in which I could get paid to have fun. But then something dramatic happened that changed everything. In a shocking nod to the Peter principle ("In a hierarchy every employee tends to rise to his level of incompetence"), I was promoted, at the tender age of twenty-six, from director of public relations to CEO of an international Rockefeller foundation. Suddenly I went from sending out press releases and writing speeches to managing a staff, putting together a budget, and reporting to a board of directors that expected me to take their fledgling foundation and turn it into a global leader. However, I had no real business experience or any clear idea about how to run a successful business. I figured out pretty quickly that I needed to figure something out pretty quickly.

In my desperation, I turned to the only person I could think of who might be able to help me: Tom Peters. Well, not Tom himself, but I did buy his book written with Robert Waterman, *In Search of Excellence*, and devoured it. In my total naiveté (this was the first business book I had ever read), I believed every word Peters and Waterman put in the book and went about dutifully attempting to implement every one of their prescriptions for business excellence. Nobody told me it was impossible, so I just went out and did it. The results were amazing. The foundation began to grow, we started getting great press, we expanded to other countries, we won some awards, and at age twenty-eight, I was nominated by the readers of *Florida Trend Magazine* as one of the top CEOs in the state of Florida under the age of forty. (Eventually I met Tom Peters in person and thanked him for his help.)

After several years at the helm of the foundation, I decided it was time for a new challenge and accepted an offer to join a leading training firm that specialized in teaching strategic account planning to sales teams at major companies. My business learning went into hyperdrive. Now it was my job to know, understand, and be able to apply dozens of cutting-edge business tools and theories. I was expected to read all of the latest business books and periodicals and attend numerous seminars and training sessions every year. I then took all of this raw knowledge and spent as many as 220 days a year on the road running from client to client and doing everything I could to help them apply all of these great ideas to achieve a higher level of business success.

In 1994, I left that firm to form my own training and consulting company, and I have been at it ever since. My library consists of more than two thousand business books, and my client list exceeds three hundred companies worldwide. I have had the chance to work with businesspeople in Japan, Hong Kong, Germany, Austria, Canada, and Mexico and nearly every state in the United States. And though it has been a total blast, I have always wondered, as I drive through small towns and look at the little shops and small companies, "Who is helping *them?*" When I attend a chamber of commerce meeting and listen to the business owners complain about their challenges and difficulties in running a profitable company, I think to myself, "But, wait, it's not supposed to be hard; it's supposed to be FUN!" When I give a speech at a national meeting for a Fortune 500 firm and listen as the managers lament how confused and stressed they are in attempting to keep their part of the business on track and running smoothly, I keep asking myself the same question: "Don't they understand this is really very simple if you just look closely enough?" Then I answer my own question: "No, they don't understand because they don't have the time to look closely. They are spending every waking minute just trying to keep up, trying to stay in the race, trying to keep their jobs."

I remind myself that it has taken me almost two decades and hundreds of thousands of pages to figure it out—time these folks do not have. They need help, and they need it right now. They need to make payroll, develop a new product, enter a new market today. So I wrote this book for them—and for you. I'm on your team now, here to help, guide, and mentor you on how to make your business as successful as possible. I'm going to share with you my best ideas, tools, and resources for making the often complex and stressful task of leading an organization as simple and enjoyable for you as it can be. I'm going to help you take a hard look at your business, and together we will develop specific plans and action steps that will allow you to dramatically improve the success of your company.

What's Inside This Book

Each of the six main chapters covers one of the core principles, with a conclusion at the end to help you take everything you've learned throughout this book and turn it into positive action in your organization right away.

Chapter One begins with the crux of any organization, though it's something that many still do not do effectively: communicating a clear, vivid, compelling, and inspiring vision for the future of the business. Whether you lead three people on a sales team or ten thousand people across the globe, one of the fundamental aspects of creating a successful enterprise is giving people the comfort, safety, and confidence of an ennobling and positive vision of its future. This is especially true in times of great turmoil and change, which many businesses are facing right now and likely will for years to come.

Chapter Two can catapult an organization to a higher level of success with one powerful idea: turning your organization into a talent magnet. We live in a knowledge economy. Very few businesses gain sustainable competitive advantage through proprietary technology, manufacturing might, or specialized logistics. One key to success for every business is to create a corporate culture that attracts, grows, and keeps the best people. This does not mean that every person who works for you needs to have three advanced degrees from Harvard and ten years as a former astronaut, only that each be the absolute best for the position that he or she is in—the best chief financial officer, the best engineer, the best receptionist, the best janitor. Obviously the skill levels of these four people are completely different, but the attitude, passion, creativity, innovation, and driving desire for success and excellence should be no different. In this chapter, we take a close look at exactly what is required to win the war for talent.

Chapter Three turns to the single biggest issue I face with all my clients worldwide: the lack of open, honest, robust, and courageous communication. If talent, innovation, and extreme customer focus are the main drivers of success for your company, a fundamental element in making sure your organization runs well is ensuring that you have superb communications across all parts of the organization and to all stakeholders. The aim of this chapter is to simplify this and give you lots of real tools to help you personally improve your communication skills.

Chapter Four explores the need for speed: how to create a culture with a strong sense of urgency. The business world has never moved faster than right now, and we can expect the pressure only to increase. Speed, agility, and proactivity are necessary requirements for survival and success—yet they cannot be pursued at the expense of disciplined execution and consistent quality. In this chapter, I share my best ideas on decision making, risk analysis, empowerment, and the value of building a vast network of people who want to help you succeed.

In Chapter Five, we study what it takes to build a performance-oriented culture that demands flawless execution. Truly great companies do not tolerate mediocrity. They set clear, ambitious, yet realistic goals and high standards of performance, and then they hold people 100 percent accountable for meeting those standards and delivering on their commitments. Refusing to accept mediocrity isn't easy and takes a lot of discipline, but it is an indispensable part of building a highly successful organization. Because this is such a huge problem in most companies I work with, a large part of this chapter is devoted to giving specific examples and instructions on how to create a culture of disciplined execution.

Chapter Six puts forth an idea that is imperative to a company's success: you must own the voice of the customer by creating a strong and trusting bond with your customers and listening to what they want from you and your business. This level of customer focus, which allows you to understand your customers as well as or better than they understand themselves, is the final principle that ties all six together. In a world of nearly limitless product options and highly educated consumers with instant access to every bit of data on price, features, and benefits of almost every product, delivering consistently superior customer service is one of the few differentiators left for creating loyal and engaged customers, which is absolutely essential for building a sustainable and highly profitable business.

Finally, in the Conclusion, I help you close the knowing-doing gap and apply the ideas you have learned. As you read the following chapters, you're going to encounter incredibly valuable ideas and tools. The Conclusion will be all about how to make sure you turn the ideas in this book into positive action in your business.

No matter how well you learn and apply the ideas in this book, there are a few elemental factors that have to happen right in every business in order to stay in business. They are the table stakes, the minimum price of admission to enter the game.

The first one is, at the very least, that you must produce a high-quality product or service. If what you sell is not worth buying, no amount of good ideas, cool strategies, or slick marketing will help you. Oh, you may be able to sell an unproven substandard product for a short time, but eventually the marketplace will punish you. All *sustainable* business success is built on delivering real value to the customer.

The next given is that you need to have a solid handle on your financials. I love the old saying that if you aren't managing your cash flow, you won't be managing much for long. Even great companies—companies with amazing products, outrageously good services, loyal customers, and fantastic strategies—have been reduced to ruin and driven to bankruptcy by poor financial management.

The last given is that change is inevitable. No single strategy will carry your company forever. Just ask Tom Peters and Robert Waterman. I used their *In Search of Excellence* as my business bible back in 1982. But ten years later, more than half of the companies they highlighted had gone out of business. Markets shift, consumer preferences change, new competitors appear, technology advances—and so must you.

If you have addressed these three issues of high-quality products and services, strong financial management, and the willingness to embrace change, you have laid the groundwork that will allow you to take the principles in this book and build the foundation for creating long-lasting success in your organization. If you are struggling with any of these, you'll still learn a great deal from this book, but your organization is at a serious disadvantage. I urge you to stay focused on fixing these problems in order to set yourself up for success.

How to Use This Book

This book is meant to be used as a tool. And like any other good tool, it adds value only if you use it. That is why on every page I strive for simplicity and usefulness. I'm not going to bog you down with a ton of research findings, multilayered theories, or extravagant Gantt charts and histograms. I'm going for making it easy to understand and easy to apply so you can enjoy the benefits of this material from the start. If you are interested in knowing about any of the research I used in writing this book, go to www.awesomelysimple.com, where you'll find references for all of the research I quote. You'll also find lots of other resources and support, such as suggested reading lists, organizational audits, workshops, and discussion questions—all designed to help you successfully implement the ideas and prescriptions in this book.

I have kept the chapters short and to the point, with clear examples and real-life stories to support the ideas I'm sharing. At the end of every chapter is a summary of the key ideas in that chapter, along with a selection of audits, questions to answer, examples, and case studies. I believe that the more ways you look at something, the more things you can learn from it, so I've provided lots of different ways to understand and, most important, apply the key themes of this book.

There are two ways to use this book for maximum impact.

The first is to read and study the book carefully. Underline important points. Make notes in the margin. Take the audits, and be brutally honest with yourself when answering the questions at the end of each chapter. When you have completed the entire book, go back and review the scores you gave on the audits, the answers to the chapter questions, and any notes you wrote, and look for patterns. My guess is that you will be able to see a distinct pattern in the areas in which your organization does well and the areas in need of improvement. This should give you some valuable guidance on exactly what you need to do to advance your organization. In the final chapter, I help you create a list of specific and measurable action steps based on what you have just learned. In this way, the book will serve as a mentor and coach, helping you to dramatically improve the way you run your business.

I have also written this book so it can be a wonderful tool for a team to work through together. Whether you're part of a handful of people running a small business, a marketing team, a product development team, or the senior management team of a large company, reading the book and going through all of the audits and questions together can be a powerful exercise to promote positive change in your organization. The first step is to get everyone in the group to not just read but carefully study the material in the book. Next, everyone on the team completes the audits and fills out the questions at the end of each chapter from his or her own point of view. At this point, you have two options. Option 1 is to sit down with your entire team and talk about what people learned, what their scores were, and how they answered the questions, which will surely drive a spirited and deeply valuable discussion. This approach is all about opening up the lines of communication and getting the team to talk about the six principles of business success, their impact on the business, and what to do about what they have discovered. Option 2, my preference, is to break your team up into small groups of three to six members, and let each group compare and contrast the lessons learned, audit scores, and their answers to the chapter questions in these small, independent teams. You want each team to identify your organization's strengths and weaknesses and the key strategies they feel they should focus on, and make a list of five recommendations on how to improve the organization. Once they have completed this work, have each team present its findings to the other teams. Typically a pattern emerges. Everyone in the room will quickly identify the organization's top strengths, biggest weaknesses, and what its areas of focus should be. Once all of the recommendations are combined, you'll have a list of priority actions that can be implemented immediately. (You will find a more detailed explanation of how to run a team workshop, downloadable copies of the various audits

audits and questions, and other resources to help you at www. awesomelysimple.com.)

This book is just the beginning of a conversation—a conversation inside your company, a conversation with me, and a conversation with other businesspeople who, like you, are striving to build truly successful organizations. To keep that conversation going, I also have a blog and discussion board on my Web site where you can post questions to me and other readers, offer advice, and share your success stories and how you used this book to help your business, so even after you finish reading the book, there will still be more help and support available to you.

It has taken nearly half of my life spent reading, studying, watching, learning, and questioning to discover that what seems so complex is actually quite simple. In this book, I share with you everything I have learned on my journey in an effort to help make yours as smooth, comfortable, and enjoyable as possible. I promise you that if you read this book carefully and apply the ideas set out here, they will have a dramatic positive impact on your business and your life. I truly wish you every success.

CHAPTER 1

Vivid Vision

A COMPELLING VISION OF WHAT YOU ARE
TRYING TO ACHIEVE THAT IS EXCEPTIONALLY WELL
COMMUNICATED TO EVERYONE INVOLVED

Having a clear, vivid, and compelling vision, the first principle of business success, is without question an essential component in building a successful company. In fact, most organizations fall down not in creating the vision but in what they do with it. Before I get into that, I want to clarify some terminology and then delve into the fundamentals of how to create a vision and why having one is so important.

Basic Terminology

Vision, mission, purpose, core values, and *guiding principles.* What do these all mean?

I get asked this question a lot, and for good reason, because different people use completely different terms to talk about the same basic information. If you went to the Internet and pulled up the vision statements of a dozen companies, you'd quickly realize that what one company says is its vision, another one calls its mission and the third one its guiding principles. Although I have worked with hundreds of organizations in establishing mission, vision, and values statements, I try not to get too hung up on the precise definitions of these words. Nevertheless, some common definitions make these terms clear.

A *mission statement* describes what an organization is all about: its purpose and primary objectives. It answers three key questions:

- Whom do we serve?
- What is the benefit to our stakeholders, community, and the world?
- Why does this organization exist?

It should resonate with all members of the organization and help them feel proud and excited to be a part of something bigger than themselves. For example, Medtronic's mission statement is ennobling and inspiring: "To contribute to human welfare by application of biomedical engineering in the research, design, manufacture, and sale of instruments or appliances that alleviate pain, restore health, and extend life."

A *vision statement* is what the organization wants to become. It is a picture of the desired future, where leaders see the business twenty years from now.

A *values statement* outlines the core beliefs, behaviors, and commitments of an organization. Values are not created; they are discovered. They are codified from the value systems and behaviors of the leaders and employees in the organization.

To sum up, a mission statement gives the overall purpose of the organization, the vision statement describes how the future will look if the organization achieves its mission, and the values statement is a code of conduct. Here is an example of what the vision, mission, and values statement might look like for a hospital:

Our Mission
To provide exceptional patient care in a compassionate and nurturing environment supported by dedicated health care professionals who strive to advance the care and treatment of the sick through advanced medical research and discoveries

Our Vision
World-class patient care through clinical excellence

Our Core Values
Compassion
Safety
Professional excellence
Embracing diversity
Complete honesty and integrity
Innovation through knowledge sharing and teamwork

I have seen a lot of time and money wasted watching companies debate the definitions of these words. And many try to craft their mission/vision/values statements so perfectly, so all-inclusively, that they never get written. This is not a contest to see who gets an A+ from the teacher for writing a great haiku. If you have the skills to create a truly elegant vision and corporate values statement, fantastic. I applaud you. But if you just put a few simple words down on a piece of paper, and they are powerful and create strong meaning and motivation for you and your people, that's fine too. The point is that the clarity of meaning and direction throughout the organization is driven by the clarity of the mission/vision/values statement. In far too many companies, these statements are ambiguous, uninspiring, and literally without meaning. The ultimate test of any statement of vision, mission, values, guiding principles, core beliefs, organizational credo—-whatever you want to call it—is its effectiveness in mobilizing people to an inspiring purpose and shared direction.

The Fundamentals of Creating a Vision

A true vision is an exciting, focused, realistic, and inspiring picture of what you and everyone else in your organization are trying to accomplish together. It's the reason you come to work every day, the impact you want to make on the world, the kind of company and products you aspire to build, the major strategies that make up the core focus of your business. Your vision does not have to be a Pulitzer Prize–winning literary masterpiece; it simply needs to be something that everyone can clearly understand and that people are honestly excited about pursuing.

I do not belong to the camp that says a vision must be specific, detailed, and measurable. I love visions that are highly detailed; they work well, and they give people a valuable idea of where they are going. But I have also seen some really successful businesses (often in high technology, in which the velocity of change is overwhelming) whose vision statements are more about how they do business and what is most important to drive success than they are about revenues or market share. I really like the way well-known business guru Guy Kawasaki approaches the idea of vision. He says that rather than creating a long and convoluted statement that nobody understands or can remember, a good vision should be like a mantra: a few words, a simple phrase that can be repeated over and over again to keep people focused on the goal. I have one client whose vision is focused on building a superior *team* that delivers real value through elegant *solutions* for its customers and looks for appropriate *growth* opportunities. These three ideas—team, solutions, and growth—have taken this firm from $50 million to $250 million in just a few years. That's a successful vision.

So the goal is to create a vision statement that is straightforward and easy to remember. As the leader, you might sit down and, after long hours of thought and scribbling, develop the vision statement for your organization (whether it is a small team or multinational company) completely on your own. Or you might consider involving a number of your key people, maybe even your entire organization, in order to get as much buy-in and support for the vision as possible. But at the end of the day, the only thing that matters is that you have a vision that people believe and are committed to, a statement that keeps your employees focused and energized to move the company forward toward a destination they are all excited about reaching.

A vision is vital to giving people a sense of security and direction. With the flattening of organizations, it's important that empowered people have a guiding destination to help them frame their decisions. Your people want to know what is most important. The vision says, in effect, *Don't worry. We know what we're doing, and we know where we're going. If we all go in this direction together, everything will turn out just fine.* In organizations that do not have a clear vision or the vision is not well communicated, there is an overwhelming sense of anxiety because people are unsure of their future. Sure, employees come to work every day, but they're not confident in exactly what they're trying to accomplish with regard to the big picture. There is unease and tension because they have no common direction, no common purpose. If that's not bad enough, lack of the well-communicated vision typically leads to a massive waste of time, money, talent, and motivation, a sure way to run any company into the ground.

Creating a vivid and compelling vision of the future is one of the most important ways for you to help your team work together toward a common goal. Another valuable tool is the creation of a set of corporate values: a list of the fundamental beliefs of your organization. They establish the rules of conduct: what is acceptable and what is not acceptable behavior within your company. If the vision is about why your organization is in business, the values are about how you will all do business together. Having a set of clear corporate values gives everyone in your organization a sense of dignity, a shared credo that reflects how they feel about themselves as professionals, about the organization they work for, and how they will interact with your stakeholders, your community, and the world.

Several years ago, I was invited to give a talk on vision and values to one of the leading financial service firms in the world. For two hours, I stood before the thirteen directors of this multibillion-dollar company and shared with them my thoughts on the importance of setting a clear direction for the firm that was solidly grounded in their corporate values, which revolved around professionalism, teamwork, respect, service, and client focus. At the end of my presentation, when

I opened the floor for questions, an interesting debate ensued. One of the directors raised the issue of what to do about a top employee: he was a multimillion-dollar producer but treated other employees aggressively and rudely in his quest to deliver his stellar numbers. I turned and pointed to the wall where there was a huge brass plaque with the values of the organization written in foot-tall letters and said, "If this employee is not living your value of respect, if he is running roughshod over the rest of his team and causing significant internal strife, then regardless of how much money he generates for the firm, he either has to change his behavior or be terminated." As those last few words came out of my mouth, one of the directors literally jumped out of his chair as if someone had hit him with a cattle prod. "You have got to be kidding me," he said. "There is no way in the world I'm going to fire somebody who brings in $30 million a year." I replied, "That's fine, as long as you chisel *respect* off the values statement. But if this group of directors tells the employees that these are the values that the firm believes in yet allows people to violate them openly as long as they generate massive amounts of cash, then people will know that making money is much more important than living the values."

Given the meltdown we've seen at companies like Enron, WorldCom, and across a broad swath of financial institutions in America, it is disappointing to realize that many of these companies met their demise because they said they valued one thing and did the opposite. Therefore, if you do create a set of organizational values, integrity to those values is paramount. The first time any employee sees you or someone else from the organization violate the values without negative ramifications, all trust is destroyed. As I've personally heard

Jack Welch, former CEO of General Electric, say, "Make an honest mistake, screw up a project, lose a million dollars on a risky business bet . . . no problem, we can fix that. But violate the values, and you're gone immediately."

The vision tells people where you want to go. The values tell them how to behave along the way. It is essential to have a clear vision and compelling values in order to run a successful organization. Now let's turn to where even companies that have a great vision and solid values often make a huge mistake.

Communicating the Vision

For a number of years, I've been doing work for an organization that brings together CEOs, presidents, and key employees at noncompetitive companies for a monthly roundtable meeting to help each other with their businesses. For the first few hours, a guest speaker addresses some critical area of business. In the afternoon, these high-level executives—most running companies between $2 million and $50 million—discuss how they will hold each other accountable for implementing the ideas they have learned. Through this work, I've had the great pleasure of presenting classes on strategic thinking and business excellence to almost nine hundred senior executives. At the end of each session, I always ask the group the same question: "What are the four biggest issues that you are dealing with right now in your company?" As they share their answers, I am always amazed because just about all of them say they are struggling with the same four basic issues. Here is the list, with an example of how they describe them to me. See if these sound familiar to you:

1. *Communicating vision.* "I have a clear vision of where I'm trying to take my organization. I think about it all the time and it's always on my mind, but I bet if you went two levels down in my company and asked people what the vision of our organization is . . . they would not be able to tell you. I realize now that even though I focus on the vision and our key strategies constantly, I have not done a good enough job of clearly communicating them throughout my entire organization."

2. *Openly addressing challenges.* "I realize now that we're not having the tough conversations we need to have in our organization. There are issues, challenges, and problems that everyone knows about but no one wants to talk about. It's the elephant in the middle of the room in every meeting. People sit and stare at each other but are unwilling to broach the subject, put it on the table, and talk about these major issues that need to be addressed. As a leader, I now understand that I'm going to have to be much more courageous in my communication and accept that it is my role to engage everyone in discussing the undiscussable."

3. *Enabling mediocrity.* "I have a few mediocre people in key places in my organization. And I understand that every day I allow them to come to work and do a poor job, turn things in late, mess up projects, and miss deadlines is another day that I am telling all of the rest of the people in my organization that I was just kidding about excellence. That if Tom or Sue or Mary is clearly incompetent, but they get the same pay, benefits, and vacation as everyone else, then that level of

mediocre performance is completely acceptable in our organization."

4. *Following through on plans.* "We have a serious problem with lack of execution. We have innovative ideas, good plans. We understand how to differentiate ourselves in the marketplace, but at the end of every year, I look back and realize that we accomplished only a fraction of what we set out to do. We have goals and objectives, but we lack the discipline to follow through and ensure that our good intentions become focused action."

I address the last three items in other chapters in this book, but let's tackle number one here: communicating the vision.

I once had a president of the company ask me, "When do you know that you have communicated the vision enough?" My answer to him was, "When you are so sick and tired of talking about the vision that you feel like you might become nauseous if you have to discuss it one more time. Then you have just started. Because at that point, the lowest-level person in your organization just heard the vision for the very first time." I cannot state this strongly enough: overcommunication of the vision and values is critical. In board meetings, through e-mail, at off-site meetings, in phone conversations, in the company newsletter, as screen savers, in one-on-one meetings, at all-hands meetings: in every conceivable communications channel, you must relentlessly communicate a clear and consistent message about the vision and future direction of your organization and the values that can never be violated. Let me give you a great example of how two of my clients in the health care industry powerfully communicate their mission, vision, and values to people across their organizations.

If you were to drive onto the San Francisco campus of the biotech company Genentech, the first thing you would notice are the massive (two- and three-story tall) pictures of real patients who have benefited from the drugs Genentech has developed. Everywhere you look are giant smiling faces reminding everyone at Genentech exactly why they come to work every day, that what they do is very important, and that their mission is about saving lives and taking care of people. At Abbott Labs, the kick-off of almost every major meeting starts with a video of a patient or doctor talking about how the work of the people at Abbott has affected his or her life. Often these events include a speech from a patient, eyes filled with tears as he or she looks out over the audience of Abbott employees and personally thanks them for saving his or her life or the life of his or her child. At the end of these stories there is not a dry eye in the room. And there is also absolutely no question why the organization exists, whom they serve, or if the work they do is important.

Finding and sharing stories like these is perhaps the best way to communicate the vision, mission, and values of your organization too. I understand that it is a bit easier for a drug company or hospital to communicate a powerfully touching life-or-death story, but every business can find a unique way to share a meaningful story with employees about how what they do every day makes a difference in the lives of their customers and community. The communication does not have to be complex or highly emotional. It simply needs to be real, sincere, and honest.

SUMMARY OF KEY POINTS

- A clear, vivid, compelling vision of the future of your organization (team, department, region, branch, division) is critical to keeping everyone focused on success.

- A *mission* says why the company exists, the *vision* says where we want to go, and *values* declare how we will act and behave along the way.

- The biggest problem in most organizations is not that they lack vision, but that the vision is poorly communicated throughout the organization.

- A great vision statement is like a mantra—a few key words that inspire and direct your people.

- The four biggest issues for many business leaders are a lack of well-communicated vision, lack of courageous communication, toleration of mediocrity, and poor execution of key plans and ideas.

EFFECTIVENESS AUDIT

This brief audit will help you determine how well your organization is doing on the key items outlined in this chapter. It is essential that you be completely honest in scoring the questions. This is not an exercise to get the highest score; it is a diagnostic tool to discover areas that need focus and improvement. Score the following statements on a scale of 1 to 10, with 1 being strongly disagree and 10 being strongly agree.

1. We have a clear, vivid, and compelling vision that is extremely well communicated throughout our entire organization. _____

2. Our organization has a deeply held set of guiding principles and core values that drives every aspect of how we do business. _____

3. We do not allow anyone to consistently violate the values and remain employed in this organization. _____

4. There is a strong and focused shared sense of direction throughout the entire organization. _____

5. Everyone in this company understands exactly why this organization exists and what we are trying to accomplish. _____

6. People throughout the organization are inspired by our mission and vision._____

EFFECTIVENESS AUDIT SCORING KEY

- A score of 9 or 10 indicates strength in your organization.

- A score of 7 or 8 is a good score but has room for improvement.

- A score of 5 or 6 is an area of concern. This score needs to be brought up because if it heads in the other direction, it could lead to serious issues.

- A score of 3 or 4 is in the danger zone and requires attention and resources to get it moving up the scale quickly.

- A score of 1 or 2 is an emergency and should be dealt with immediately.

THINGS TO THINK ABOUT AND DISCUSS

It is important to take time and give the following questions some serious thought. Be honest with yourself, and think your answers through in detail. You might also find it valuable to gather several people from your organization to discuss these questions as a group, exploring how each of you might answer the same questions differently. These opposing points of view and alternative ideas are critical to developing quality answers.

1. What is the mission of our organization? Why do we exist? What is the noble purpose we are fulfilling?

2. Who in society would suffer, other than our employees, if our organization went out of business?

3. What is the vision for our organization? What are we trying to build? Where would we like to see this company five, ten, and twenty years into the future?

4. What are the core values of our organization? What are our most deeply held beliefs about the way we want to behave?

5. What are our spoken and unspoken rules about excellence, teamwork, quality, customer focus, professionalism, communication, accountability, corporate culture, and corporate responsibility?

6. How do we want our organization to be viewed from the outside? What words would we like our customers to use when describing our company? What feelings and emotions would we like our various stakeholders to have about our company?

7. What sort of a legacy do we want to leave in the communities where we work?

TURNING IDEAS INTO ACTION

Here are several suggestions on how you can take some of the main ideas of this chapter and begin to implement them immediately. Some of them might work perfectly for you; others will need some adjustment and customization. Read them carefully, and start thinking about how you can make them work in your organization.

1. If you do not already have them, create mission, vision, and values statements. This can be done independently by the leader of the organization or a committee of key people who are enthusiastic about working on this project, or you can solicit feedback from the entire organization. Typically it is best to get as much feedback as possible from various stakeholders and then have two or three key people create a draft document that can be circulated for comments. It is important to let people have a voice in the process so that they feel that they have some ownership in

the final document and will therefore be much more committed to the mission, vision, and values.

2. If you do have mission, vision, and values statements in place, survey your employees to see if they know and understand the statements and if they consider them relevant to and resonant with the organization. The only way these statements can be effective is if people honestly believe in them and strive every day to live them.

3. Survey your customers to gather their feelings and attitudes about your mission, vision, and values. Do they resonate with your customers as the kind of business they want to support and believe that you are? In your customers' eyes, is your organization living your stated mission, vision, and values?

4. Develop a specific, measurable, and comprehensive communications plan for ensuring that the mission, vision, and values are effectively communicated throughout all levels of the organization and to key stakeholders. Measure the success of this program through surveys and one-on-one meetings at least twice a year.

5. Create a formal reward and recognition program for employees who live the values and support the mission and vision. These can be things like employee of the month award, employee of the year award, a special parking space, a day off, a cash bonus, a small gift certificate, flextime, a donation to the employee's favorite charity, a plaque or award, a handwritten note from the CEO thanking the employee for his or her dedication and commitment to the mission, vision, and values—the options are endless. The idea is to reward employees with something they value, and do so publicly and sincerely.

6. Find innovative ways to tie your mission, vision, and values with community outreach, charitable support, and sustainable business practices.

7. Refuse to tolerate any violation of the values. Make it clear that prudent risk taking or failing at something new or challenging is absolutely acceptable; it is even rewarded. But violating one of the core values will result in immediate termination.

If you are finding it challenging to come up with a mission, vision, or values statement, here are two excellent examples to help get your gears turning. The first is a traditionally written mission, vision, and values statement from the City of Oklahoma City. This document clearly articulates exactly what the city leaders are trying to achieve for their community. The second example is from one of my favorite restaurants in the world, the Dragonfly Sushi and Sake Company, in my home town of Gainesville, Florida. This award-winning establishment is a shining example of the power of a vivid and compelling vision and mission that is woven into every element of the business and throughout the culture of the entire organization.

The City of Oklahoma City Mission, Vision, and Values Statements

Mission Statement
The City of Oklahoma City's mission is to provide the leadership, commitment and resources to achieve our vision by:

Offering a clean, safe and affordable City.
Providing well-managed and maintained infrastructure through proactive and reactive services, excellent stewardship of public assets and a variety of cultural, recreational and entertainment opportunities that enhance the quality of life.
Creating and maintaining effective partnerships to promote employment opportunities and individual and business success.
Advancing a model of professionalism that ensures the delivery of high-quality products and services, continuously improves efficiency and removes barriers for future development.

Vision Statement
Oklahoma City is a safe, clean, affordable City. We are a family-friendly community of strong moral character, solid values and a caring spirit. We strive to provide the right balance of cosmopolitan and rural areas by offering a well-planned and growing community that focuses on a wide variety of business, educational, cultural, entertainment and recreational opportunities. We are a diverse, friendly City that encourages individuality and excellence.

Mission, Vision, and Values Statements

We are The City of Oklahoma City.

Public Service is our purpose. It is why we are here. We commit to provide competent, dependable and efficient service to all by knowing our jobs and our City.

We value dependability and accountability in our relationships.

We value tactful, useful, informative and honest communication among ourselves and with our community. Listening to the needs of others is a critical part of our communication process.

We honor diversity by respecting our customers and fellow employees.

We commit to continuous improvement and growth through visionary, proactive leadership and technology.

We set these standards of quality service by upholding our core values.

We are The City of Oklahoma City.

Dragonfly Sushi & Sake Company Mission Statement

We strive to be excellent through exceeding our guests' expectations by providing a dining experience that is Sensual, Spiritual and Savory.

Vision

To be the restaurant of choice for Japanese cuisine in the Gainesville area.

The Credo

Always strive to be excellent by exemplifying the Bushido and treating all team members and guests with care, understanding, respect and fairness.

Culture Statement

Our corporate culture is about passionate people who are focused and committed to Absolute Hospitality so we may become the very best in our industry. Absolute Hospitality means taking care of each other first, then our guests, then our vendors, and lastly our shareholders. We believe through Absolute Hospitality, we can continue to achieve professional success as well as personal success.

For more resources on creating mission, vision, and values statements, go to www.awesomelysimple.com.

The mission, vision, and values (M/V/V) can be communicated in a number of ways—for example:

- Create posters, plaques, and banners.

- Create T-shirts, hats, pens, key chains, screen savers, mouse pads, and buttons with the M/V/V statements.

- Develop a company newsletter or blog.

- Have senior executives, managers, or customers present a speech or write an article.

- Circulate stories about how employees live the M/V/V.

- Print the M/V/V on agendas, and open meetings with a discussion of them.

- Make sure the M/V/V are included as part of all strategic, operational, and tactical plans.

- Spend time talking about the M/V/V and key strategies at all-hands and town hall meetings.

- Use the M/V/V as themes for national meetings, sales meetings, and management meetings.

- Create formal and informal recognition programs to reward people who exemplify living the M/V/V.

- From time to time, leave a message about the M/V/V to all employees on their voice mail or through e-mail.

- Create a committee that surveys employees and keeps the M/V/V fresh and relevant.

- Bring in customers once or twice a year to talk to employees about how the company's M/V/V have touched them and made their lives better.

Always remember that all of this is useless if you do not actually live the mission, vision, and values throughout the entire organization. The truth is, if you've created a noble mission, a compelling vision, and a set of deeply held values, you should be excited to tell everyone about them. Communicating the vision should never feel like a chore; it should be motivating and inspiring to share your feelings and excitement about the future of the company. Plaques, speeches, and banners are nice, but passion is what brings people together and makes things happen.

One Last Word on Communicating the Vision

I've supplied a list of possibilities, but the most important part of communicating the vision is doing it authentically. As a leader, it is vital to let people know, in whatever way you find most comfortable, that you are truly passionate about the mission, vision, and values of your organization. Different leaders do this in different ways. Some use what is called symbol management, looking for little ways to send a clear message about what they are focused on in the business and what values they hold most deeply. An example is the manager of a large hotel who stops to pick up trash in the parking lot on the way into the lobby, or a customer service manager who answers her own phone by the second ring to demonstrate that responsiveness is critical. These small acts send big messages. Some leaders give inspiring speeches to rally the troops, while others prefer a more personal approach. For example, I think best by writing things down, so whenever I have something important to say, I write a memo about the ideas I want folks to focus on. Typically these memos are five or six pages long, and I e-mail them to everyone on my team and then invite them to visit me in my office at their convenience to sit down and discuss the memo and answer any questions they might have. I do this only once or twice a year, but I try as hard as I can to speak from my heart and really tell the people who work with me what I feel are the most essential things for us to focus on in order to enjoy the level of success we all want to achieve together. The memos are personal and honest and have been extremely effective. (If you would like to read an example of one of my memos, go to: www.awesomelysimple.com.)

CHAPTER 2

Best People

HIGHLY TALENTED INDIVIDUALS WHO ARE ALSO MASTERS OF COLLABORATION

I want to share an idea with you that can completely shift the future of your company, an idea so important that without it, there is virtually no way to build a great organization. Unbelievably, far too few businesses understand the importance of this very simple fact: *the future of your company is directly tied to the quality of talent you can attract and keep.*

I know that doesn't sound particularly earth shattering, sexy, or revolutionary, but it underlies one of the most powerful business paradoxes I have encountered. Every business book I buy, every business magazine I read, and literally thousands of research studies clearly demonstrate that no organization can survive unless one of their major strategies revolves around talent management. Yet it has been my frustrating experience that not nearly enough businesses take it seriously. Oh, some pay a lot of lip-service to the "it's a war for talent" story, but I have found that it is the very rare company that truly embraces the idea of finding, hiring, and taking care of only the very best people they can possibly bring into the organization. This is great for you, because if your organization makes talent acquisition and development a core competency, you will have a huge competitive advantage.

Let's face up to reality. Products across the globe—even those that traditionally have been considered unique and valuable—are becoming commoditized. Every company, in every industry, is feeling the squeeze of increased competition and extremely well-informed consumers who have unprecedented access to the information needed to make a buying decision. The old bastions of competitive advantage—location, access to capital, proprietary technology, distribution channels, and others—are in most cases no longer relevant. To my mind, the only truly sustainable competitive advantage left is the creation of a corporate culture that is solidly built on a foundation of continuous innovation and extreme customer focus—both of which can be delivered only by highly talented people.

Here is the formula for business success in the future:

Talent $\times$ Culture = Profit.

Find and Keep Top Talent

The word *talent* can encompass numerous meanings, so here is what I mean when I think about what constitutes real business talent:

The Five C's of Talent

1. *Competence.* At the very foundation, to be considered "talented," a person has to be highly competent in an

area that is valuable in the marketplace. This person must possess skills, abilities, ideas, and information that others are willing to pay for. Truly talented people are fanatics for lifelong learning, with an insatiable desire to increase their skills and knowledge at every possible opportunity. Through books, magazines, CDs, podcasts, seminars, and mentors, every successful businessperson is a sponge for new ideas.

2. *Character.* You can have the smartest person on your team, the very highest performer—yet if he or she isn't completely trustworthy, you have a liability, not an asset. It is absolutely essential to business success that the talented people you hire conduct themselves with complete integrity in every situation. Honesty, transparency, and living a values-based life are the elements that build professional and personal character.

3. *Collaboration.* The world is too complex, with too much information, and moving at too high a velocity for any single individual to handle it alone. (Even the Lone Ranger had Tonto.) For talented individuals to be effective in any organization, they must be superb at collaborating with others, work well on teams, engage widely in knowledge sharing, and be willing to submerge their personal egos for the success of those around them. Teamwork is mandatory, not optional.

4. *Communication.* Every talented business professional who succeeds at a high level is an expert communicator. But contrary to what you might be thinking, it is not great skills of oratory or persuasion that are the most important, but rather the ability to ask superior

questions and then listen to the answers. Truly great communicators are curious. They watch everything, listen to every word, look for the meaning and emotions behind the words, and make the person they are talking to the very center of their universe at that moment. They are adept at laying out simple, clear, and logical arguments—all while connecting emotionally. Talented businesspeople understand that communications skills like clear speech, focused listening, asking questions, body language, motivation, and conflict resolution are skills that must be developed and constantly improved.

5. *Commitment.* No great success is ever achieved without great effort. Highly talented businesspeople are committed, driven, and passionate about what they are doing. They do not see their work as a job, but instead as an adventure, a quest, a higher calling. They have a positive can-do attitude, embrace risk, and see setbacks as opportunities for learning. More than charisma, it is their focused and disciplined commitment to excellence and their personal integrity that inspire those around them.

To succeed in the future, you must become a fanatic about finding and recruiting top talent. You need to be obsessed with discovering highly competent people of impeccable character who work really well with others, are great communicators, and have a driving commitment to excellence. And the only way to succeed in this challenge is to put into place the systems, processes, and programs necessary to build a pipeline that delivers a steady stream of talent to your team. Time and time again, I've had organizational leaders tell me how hard it is to find "good people." They cry in their cornflakes that it is impossible to find real talent. But when I ask these leaders to describe the programs they have in place to hunt down and land top talent, the typical reply is: "We have a help wanted ad in the newspaper and posted something on Monster.com." That is a pathetic effort. The only way to win the war for talent is to employ the Powell doctrine of "shock and awe" by making talent acquisition a major strategic thrust in your company. To get a better handle on what I mean, consider these questions:

- Do you have a list of at least ten supertalented people you'd love to hire right now if you only had a position available for them?

- Do you take one highly talented person you'd like to hire to lunch every month?

- Is there someone in your company who has a strong personal relationship with the top placement officers at all local and regional colleges and universities?

- Is there someone in your company who is attending numerous association and community meetings, constantly looking for top talent?

- Do you have open houses where you invite interested individuals to consider a career with your firm?

- Do you have an internship program that taps promising college students to come in and work with you before they are on the open market?

- Do you have a wide network of business colleagues who are constantly looking for talented individuals to refer to your company?

- Are you keeping a close eye on the talented people who work for your competition?

- Do you have a reward system for your current employees if they recommend a highly talented person who becomes a new member of your organization?

- Are you, or your human resources director, strategically looking at the needs of your organization three to five years down the road, and beginning the process of finding the type of talent you'll need long before you get in a tight situation?

- Do you have a robust, well-thought-out, and highly effective interviewing process to ensure that you are making the best possible hiring decisions?

- Do you have a clear and focused competency model of exactly the skill sets, attitudes, and behaviors you are looking for in the kind of people you want to bring onto your team?

- Do you have a well-thought-out and focused exit interview process you employ for every person who leaves your organization?

There are many more questions I could ask (go to www. awesomelysimple.com for additional resources), but this sampling gives you a good idea of the basic foundation you need in place if you're going to be serious about talent acquisition. Let me give you a personal example.

More than ten years ago, I went to a local advertising firm to get a logo developed for a new executive training company I was starting. My experience with the owner of the firm was less than outstanding, but I was extremely impressed with the work that one of the designers had done, a young man named Tony DiFranco. I decided not to use that firm for any more work but kept my eye on Tony. About a year later, the owner of the new advertising firm I was using called me to let me know he was looking to hire a new creative director and was considering Tony for the job. I told him to call Tony immediately and do whatever it took to get him on board—and not to call me back until Tony was on his team. Tony joined his firm a week later.

For the next several years, I watched Tony carefully. I gave all of my business to him and recommended his services to all of my clients. I took him to lunch from time to time. I invited him and his family over for dinner. We went fishing together. I sent him books and articles that I thought he might find interesting. I sent him e-mails when I saw outstanding work he had done for other clients at his firm. For eight years, I kept Tony on my radar and stayed on his, in the hope that one day I would find a way to get him on my team.

Six years ago, the advertising firm that Tony was working for dissolved, and that was the opportunity I had been waiting for. I had found in Tony someone of incredible talent, unquestioned integrity, deep passion, and real customer focus, and I asked him to become a partner in a new strategic branding firm, one I started solely to take advantage of his amazing skills. The firm, Flycaster & Co., has been a great success. We have a small group of clients who allow us to do challenging, fun work and serve as trusted advisors to their businesses. The reason I tell you the story? I chased Tony for eleven years. For more than a decade, I watched him, talked to him, visited with him, and built a relationship that led to the founding of a new company, a profitable partnership, and a strong and rewarding personal friendship. That is what it takes if you are serious about finding the absolutely best people and getting them on your team. If you are hiring truly great people, they are usually a lot of fun to be around, so this sort of recruiting is quite enjoyable too.

Something else is essential to keep in mind as you think about the idea of building a highly talented team: talented people who do not play well in the sandbox with others, no matter how good they are at what they do, are not talent. You will hear many business leaders say, "People are our most valuable asset," but that is simply not accurate. Your *talented people* are your most valuable asset; your *worst people* are your biggest liability. This important point was hammered home for me when I was working on a project with another consultant. For two days, as I stood in the front of the room presenting to a large group of presidents and CEOs, he said nothing. Finally, at the end of the program I asked him if he had anything he might like to contribute. He stood up and walked to the front of the room, then said, "When you get back to your office, take a look around your company, and find your lowest-performing employee. Then realize that this is the person who sets the standard of acceptable performance for your entire organization." The folks in the room were floored at this profound (and, for some of them, painful) point. I know that it is no coincidence that every wildly successful businessperson I've ever worked with has had the same philosophy: "I just figured I'd hire people who were smarter than me, and everything would work out all right."

I cannot stress this point strongly enough: the companies that survive and thrive in the future will be the ones that treat talent acquisition, development, and retention as a major strategic imperative. Then they will hold those talented individuals fully accountable for being superior at collaboration and knowledge sharing, and they will be highly effective team players. Now that we have addressed the first part of the business success equation, talent, it is time to look at the other critical element in the formula: culture.

Creating a Winning Culture

The evidence is overwhelming and irrefutable. In hundreds of studies, carried out in thousands of companies, looking at millions of employees, the facts are clear: highly engaged employees are the single greatest driver of customer satisfaction and loyalty, which is in turn the number one driver of organizational profitability and long-term success. Put another way: happy employees lead to happy customers and higher profits. How much higher? The findings range from 104 to 320 percent higher, but no matter how you look at it, taking good care of your employees so that they can take good care of your customers is a brilliant business decision.

Just what is it that creates highly engaged employees? In a word, culture. But much like the concept of talent, understanding the idea of culture, as it is used in a business context, can be a slippery issue. To me, corporate culture represents the written and unwritten rules of behavior, teamwork, values, ethics, and priorities that permeate an organization. Culture can be nurtured, supported, encouraged, and guided—but never mandated or controlled. When you walk into an organization with a great corporate culture, it is immediately evident. People are happy, the place hums, and there's a positive energy flow and excitement at every level. There is a strong sense of camaraderie, esprit de corps, and obvious pride in the products they build and the services they deliver. In organizations with a negative culture, you find turf guarding, finger pointing, politicking, and rumor mongering. Even if the financial benefits of a positive corporate culture weren't enough to convince you, it just makes sense that no one who is truly talented would want to work in an organization with a dysfunctional corporate culture.

During my career, it has been my great pleasure to work inside a number of organizations with strong positive corporate cultures such as State Farm Insurance, GE, the Mayo Clinic, and, most recently, an organization that has been recognized for having one of the best organizational cultures in America, Genentech. Based on all of the research I have studied about positive corporate culture and my years of experience working inside these leading organizations, here is a list of the key things you must focus on to build a culture that attracts and motivates top talent:

- *Meaning.* More than anything else perhaps, talented people want to feel that the work they do makes a positive difference in the world. Being number one, maximizing shareholder value, and doubling profitability are not key motivators for talent. Great people want to be in an organization where they can be proud of the challenging and important work they produce. To them, work is much more about purpose than positions, power, or profits.

- *Respect.* I have been teaching classes inside different organizations for over fifteen years, and until two years ago I never heard this word as a main component of building a strong corporate culture. Yes, respect was important, but it was nowhere near the priority it has become. Talented people want to be respected for the work they do, treated fairly, and made to feel that their voices will be heard and their opinions valued. A culture of respect and dignity is now a nonnegotiable minimum standard for people who are talented enough to have options.

- *Empowerment.* An outstanding corporate culture is one that gives clear direction through a vivid compelling vision and focused strategies, sets high standards for performance, and supports people with the training, mentoring, coaching, resources, and authority needed to succeed—and then gets out of their way and gives them the opportunity to excel by exceeding the standards and achieving the vision. Two extreme counterexamples are micromanagement and mushroom management (keeping people in the dark and covering them with manure). Both drive away talent.

- *Transparency.* Here is one of my favorite business maxims: "People without access to information do not have to take responsibility for their actions." The hallmark of any great corporate culture is high levels of open, honest, robust communication. In today's world, information is not power; sharing information is what gives you power. In a positive culture, people communicate with candor, directness, and empathy. Honesty and frankness are held as key values, and EQ (emotional quotient) is just as important as, if not more important than, IQ.

- *Fun.* This doesn't mean there are whoopee cushions under everybody's chairs and a rock climbing wall in the lobby. It means that people enjoy the work they do and the people they do it with. The organization feels like one big family. People are working with folks they genuinely like, people they consider real friends, and sometimes even their best friends. Sure, they enjoy their weekends and time off, but they also look forward to coming to work and having fun doing rewarding work with cool people.

In other words, the people who work for you are basically looking for two critical items: opportunity and appreciation—the opportunity to do meaningful work on important projects with talented people, and then sincere appreciation for their contribution.

Now go back and study the preceding list. There are two critically important ideas that you should take away from what I am telling you about building a winning culture. The first is what is NOT on the list: money. Money is not a primary driver of employee satisfaction and engagement. You must pay people fairly (whatever they would get to do a similar job at a similar organization), but beyond about 10 percent above that level, money is not a huge motivating factor for highly talented people. Here is the way it works: if you give people all of the things I have listed above and a reasonable paycheck for the work they do, you can absolutely attract the very best players. If you give them few or none of the things above but lots of money, only the greedy ones will stay (as long as you continue to increase their pay). If you give people none of the things on this list and a below-average wage, only the ones who can't get a job anyplace else will stay.

If you make your business a high-engagement, fun place to work, you can attract the best because the number one driver of attracting top talent is the extremely talented people you already have working for you, who love the company so much that they tell all of their talented friends about the cool work they do and their cool colleagues. It is not how much you pay, your benefits, or your vacation policies. Happy talent attracts more talent. And it is happy, engaged, and satisfied employees who strive to deliver the highest-quality products and services and give superior customer service (and will tolerate nothing less)—which can drive a 100 to 300 percent increase in your revenues and profitability. If that is not the secret to success, I don't know what is.

Here is the second big point from the list: it does not cost any money to do the things on the list; they are all what I call atmosphere issues. It does not cost a dime to treat people with more respect, to empower them, to try to have more open and honest communication and fun at work every day. Regardless of where you are in the organization or the size of your budget, there is nothing to stop you from embracing these ideas and building them into the culture of your organization. An example makes this point well.

Many years ago, I was asked to run some leadership and team-building sessions for a midsized company. In the early stages of the engagement, I started to get a bad sense about the culture of the company, so I decided to do an organizational effectiveness audit to see if I could better understand how people were feeling. I deployed a confidential Web-based survey to take the pulse of the organization. The results showed that it was near death. Out of hundreds of similar audits I had conducted over the years, this organization had the worst scores I had ever seen. On a scale of 1 to 10, where 10 signified "world class" and 1 signified "completely pathetic," the general scores all fell in the 1.5 to 2.3 range. For example, the score on "level of open and honest and robust communication" was 1.2; "level of trust in my coworkers" a 1.6; and "respect and trust in the senior management team" an unbelievable 0.9. And as if the scores were not bad enough, in the open comments section where I allowed people to explain their answers and voice their concerns, the feedback was horrifying. Out of a company with a little more than four hundred employees, fully 98 percent of the staff felt that the senior management team was highly incompetent, condescending, unreasonable, and unwilling to communicate openly. For their part, the management team all scored themselves with 9s and 10s.

Because the scores were so bad, I did several personal interviews to make sure I understood what was really happening. The interviews were even worse. People were angry, dispirited, and totally fed up with the management team. The management team, however, basically felt they were about as close to perfect as they could get. The mood of the employees was polarized into two camps: revolt or mass exodus. Faced with this sort of culture emergency, I decided that what was needed in this particular case was shock treatment.

I arranged for a meeting of the entire company, all four hundred employees and the management team together in the corporate cafeteria. There slide by slide, I presented the findings of the surveys and my interviews. Standing in front of all of these people, I told them that their scores were the worst I had seen and if they didn't find a way to dramatically improve morale and culture quickly, I felt that the organization would surely implode. I also pointed out that nearly every person in the room felt that the number one issue that was driving the company into the ground was that three specific individuals on the management team had personally destroyed the positive culture of the organization. As I opened up the floor for Q&A, a large gentleman dressed as though he likely worked on the loading dock said in a strong southern accent, "It used to be like one big family around here. We all got along, we helped each other, and we had fun. But it ain't like that no more." Then, pointing over toward my three new best friends on the management team, he said, "They killed it."

He went on, "We used to have this big party every year, where all the people came with their kids and their families, and we played volleyball and swam in the lake and had a big barbecue. That's when it was like family here; that's when we were all having fun and working hard for the company. But they canceled the party, said they didn't want to pay for it anymore—not that we couldn't afford it, mind you, just that they didn't want to pay for it. That's what killed our culture: when it became obvious that they cared a lot more about money than they did about us."

As he told this story and heads started to nod vigorously across the entire employee section of the audience, it was clear that many people in the room felt exactly the same way as the gentleman who had spoken up. So I said, "May I ask you a question? Do you ever take your family out to dinner?" He replied, "Yes, of course, I do." So I said, "Then why don't you just take the money you would normally spend to take your family out to dinner, and get everybody else to do the exact same thing, and put all that money together and have a giant barbecue—and don't invite those three people?" I paused for a second to let that question hang in the air and then continued, "You need to remember that there are four hundred of you and only three of them. If you want to have a great culture, if you want this place to feel like family, if you want to treat each other with respect and trust and make this an absolutely great place to work, they can't stop you. You actually have all the power. Culture is created by all of the people who work in an organization, not by the management team. If you don't like the way it feels around here, then all of you can get together and make a decision to treat each other differently—regardless of how these three people may or may not treat you." At which time, one of the three people I had just mentioned pointed at me from the front row and silently mouthed, "You're gone." Yes, I got terminated right in the middle of my speech. As I was talking, the big southern gentleman's eyes began to light up and in an excited voice, he said, "We could do that, couldn't we?" And I replied, "Yes, you could, you most certainly could." And a month later, they did. A year later, they had all but completely turned around the culture, once again making their company a great place to work (and the three managers had been, shall we say, made available to industry).

To me, this is one of the most exciting ideas in this book: no matter where you are in the organization, no matter what your title is, you have the ability to influence the culture of your organization. You can start with just the people on your team, or maybe a handful of folks from a few different departments, sitting down together and deciding that you want to make your company a better place to work. Changing the culture of an organization is not an edict that comes from on high. Great companies are built when people across the business decide that they are going to treat each other (and their customers) in such a way as to create an atmosphere of fun, respect, professionalism, innovation, and excitement while doing work that is challenging and deeply rewarding. It can start today, and it can start with you.

Leading Talent

During the past decade, I have had the honor of teaching a series of advanced programs for employees at a number of organizations who have been selected as having high potential. In companies with tens of thousands of employees, such as Pepsi, Alltel, Abbott Labs, and State Farm Insurance, the senior management team hand-picked a small group of those they felt held great promise as the organization's future leaders and sent them through an intense executive development program to prepare them for the next levels of their careers. For example, I served as one of the lead instructors for a Fortune 100 financial firm that asked me to take nineteen of its sixty-four thousand employees from around the world and run them through a six-month Global Leadership Development Program.

Whenever I am with a group of these incredibly talented individuals—people who could work at any company they wanted to—I ask them to describe for me the kind of leader they want to work for. I am curious to understand what would inspire and motivate these highly skilled employees and instill in them a sense of loyalty and commitment to the organization. Their answers are always consistent. It turns out that there are five key characteristics that highly talented people demand from their leaders:

A Great Leader Is . . .

1. Credible

    - Completely honest, transparent, and willing to speak with candor

    - Living the company's values with impeccable integrity

    - Highly competent; knows how to do the job well and has solid leadership skills

    - 100 percent accountable; keeps promises

    - Acting on a clear vision for the future of the organization

    - Passionate and excited about the work, the employees, the company, and the customers

2. Respectful

    - Open to the ideas of others and interested in what they have to say

- Treats people with dignity and embraces diversity at all levels

- Talks to people in a respectful tone

- Treats everyone fairly (not equally—but fairly)

3. Approachable

- Genuine—does not put on an act of superiority

- Maintains an open door policy and makes time to meet with people

- Practices management by wandering around and looks to catch people doing things right

- A great listener—focused, never distracted, listens intently, remembers, and cares

- High IQ and high EQ—intelligent, competent, and able to make a strong emotional connection

- Appreciative—shows genuine gratitude and thankfulness

4. A team player

- Develops and displays a high level of competence

- Follows through on all commitments and delivers results

- Demonstrates integrity by ensuring that actions and words are consistent

- Stands behind the team and fully supports team decisions

- Helps the other members of the team and is enjoyable and fun to work with

- Asks great questions, asks for help, listens, and keeps everyone informed

- Highly self-aware and willing to admit when he or she makes a mistake or does not have the answer

5. Highly professional

- Takes his or her career seriously, approaches it as a craft, strongly committed to lifelong learning

- Has a clear set of values and sets the standard for ethical behavior and integrity

- Communicates with honesty, authenticity, and transparency

- Treats everyone with respect, fairness, and dignity

- Loyal to the organization, committed to the team

- Dedicated to delivering superior service to their team and the customer

- Strives for work/life balance and helps others to do the same

As you will notice, several of these traits overlap. For example, keeping promises is just as important for being credible as it is for being an effective team member, as are excellent communication and high levels of accountability. So if you had the chance to work with several hundred people who were considered the absolute best in the organizations they work for, here is what they will tell you they are looking for in a leader they would give 110 percent of their discretionary effort to: a true professional who is credible, respectful, authentic, and a great team player. That's about as awesomely simple as I can make it.

SUMMARY OF KEY POINTS

- The future of your company is directly tied to the quality of the talent you can attract and keep.

- Although every businessperson knows that the only way to build a world-class company is with world-class employees, very few take action on this powerful idea.

- The only sustainable competitive advantage left is creating a culture of continuous innovation and extreme customer focus.

- The Five C's of talent: competence, character, collaboration, communication, and commitment.

- To be successful in talent acquisition, you must have the programs and processes in place to create a steady stream of talented people into your organization.

- The time to start looking for the talent you will need five years from now is right now.

- The most important factor in attracting and keeping highly talented people is the organization's culture.

- The culture that engages and satisfies your best people is one that revolves around fun, meaning, respect, opportunity, empowerment, and transparency.

- Highly engaged employees are the single greatest driver of customer satisfaction and loyalty, which is the number one driver of organizational profitability and long-term success.

- Talented people are willing to follow a leader who is honest, credible, approachable, authentic, respectful, professional, and a solid team player.

EFFECTIVENESS AUDIT

This brief audit will help you determine how well your organization is doing on the key items outlined in this chapter. It is essential that you be completely honest in scoring the questions. This is not an exercise to get the highest score; it is a diagnostic tool to discover areas that need focus and improvement. Score the following statements on a scale of 1 to 10, with 1 being strongly disagree and 10 being strongly agree.

1. Finding top talent is a major focus of our organization. _____

2. We have a robust program or process in place for identifying and recruiting highly talented people. _____

3. We have a thorough and well-thought-out interviewing process. ____

4. We have the kind of corporate culture that attracts top talent. _____

5. Our organization is a fun place to work, with a supportive, family-like atmosphere. _____

6. Our employees are highly engaged in making our company successful. _____

7. We have loyal and strongly engaged customers. _____

8. Our people take great pride in our organization and the work we do._

9. We have a culture that is highly respectful, embraces diversity, and treats people fairly. _____

10. We have a strong training and development program that helps people build the skills and knowledge necessary to succeed._____

11. There is a high level of open, honest, transparent communication throughout the entire organization. _____

12. People are given the direction, resources, and support they need to accomplish their tasks and then are empowered to do their best work. _____

13. The key leaders in our organization are credible, respectful, approachable, highly professional, and solid team players. _____

*   A score of 9 or 10 indicates strength in your organization.

*   A score of 7 or 8 is a good score but has room for improvement.

*   A score of 5 or 6 is an area of concern. This score needs to be
brought up because if it heads in the other direction, it could lead
to serious issues.

*   A score of 3 or 4 is in the danger zone and requires attention and
resources to get it moving up the scale quickly.

*   A score of 1 or 2 is an emergency and should be dealt with
immediately.

THINGS TO THINK ABOUT
AND DISCUSS

It is important to take time and give the following questions some serious thought. Be honest with yourself, and think your answers through in
detail. You might also find it valuable to gather several people from your
organization to discuss these questions as a group, exploring how each of
you might answer the same questions differently. These opposing points
of view and alternative ideas are critical to developing quality answers.

1. If your organization truly became a talent machine, what sort of an
impact would it have?

2. What is standing in the way of attracting top talent to your organization
right now?

3. How would you describe the current culture of your organization?

4. What is the single best attribute of your current corporate culture?

5. What is the single worst attribute of your current corporate culture?

6. How do you think your customers (internal and external) currently view your organization?

7. How would you describe the leadership style that permeates your organization: command and control; empowerment; micromanagement; people focused; money focused; lead by example; do as I say, not as I do; fair and reasonable; aggressive and demanding; and so on?

8. Why do you think respect has become such an important issue for employees?

9. Explain what it is about your organization and the work you do that would cause your employees to feel that their work was genuinely meaningful and important?

10. Do you think that the majority of employees in your organization are proud of where they work and the work they do? If so, why? If not, why not?

TURNING IDEAS INTO ACTION

Here are several suggestions on how you can take some of the main ideas of this chapter and begin to implement them immediately. Some of them might work perfectly for you; others will need some adjustment and customization. Read them carefully, and start thinking about how you can make them work in your organization.

1. If one does not already exist, create a systematic process for finding, recruiting, interviewing, and hiring the most talented people you can find.

2. Make sure that everyone involved in the interviewing process has had ample training in how to conduct effective interviews.

3. Direct and empower a key human resource person to become your new talent czar.

4. Create a competency model that clearly identifies the characteristics, skills, abilities, knowledge, and attitude you are looking for in both current and future employees.

5. Conduct a survey to assess the current culture of your organization and the level of engagement of your employees.

6. Create a formal and informal recognition and rewards program to ensure that employees feel appreciated for the work they do.

7. Establish a committee to develop innovative ways to make your workplace more fun, supportive, and friendly.

8. Encourage managers to have an open door policy, make more time to meet with their people, and practice management by walking around.

9. Whether you send small groups of employees out for skills training at a seminar, ask your top performers to teach in-house seminars and training sessions, or create an internal "university" for advanced executive education, make training and development a top priority across all layers of your organization.

CASE STUDY: INTERVIEW WITH BILL DAVIDSON, CONNOISSEUR OF TALENT

In my line of work, I meet a lot of senior executives. Some are incredibly talented, some are just average, and a rare few are truly great leaders. Bill Davidson is perhaps one of the finest leaders I've ever had the opportunity to work with. He has an uncanny ability to find and attract highly talented people and build strong, high-performance teams that become intensely loyal to him. I met Bill in the early 1990s when he was a young executive director at Bell Atlantic Mobile and I was asked to assist in delivering some sales training for his team. A few years later, Bill had moved to GE Capital, where I worked on another project with him. Today Bill is the senior vice president of global marketing and investor relations at QUALCOMM, where I assist his team in the areas of strategic thinking and scenario planning. Out of the thousands of executives I work with, Bill is the strongest I have ever met in talent identification, acquisition, and development, so I asked him to explain his secrets.

Talent Identification

"Fairly early in my career as a manager, I was given the opportunity to take a class on interviewing skills, and one thing sticks with me from that class and it has stuck with me for my entire career. . . . When most people interview candidates, they spend time verifying information. They'll say, 'Oh, so you went to Duke? Ah, and it looks like you majored in econ?' Then they'll try to test some institutional knowledge such as, 'Talk to me about the price elasticity of such and such.' The way I see it, their experience is right there on their résumé, so unless it's fraudulent, I figure you should just take that at face value.

"What the class taught me was that if you really do a good job in an interview, you find out how a candidate will react in certain situations. It's the really simple things like asking something along the line of, 'Tell me about a time when you just royally screwed up at work. Where you got caught completely flat-footed, or a customer asked you to do something and you forgot—a time where you just totally dropped the ball.' Then after they answer, you say, 'Well, what did you do to recover? How did you build the relationship back up?' You really want to dig in and see what makes these people tick; you're trying to gauge what I call wisdom versus intellect.

"I definitely want smart people on my team, but I also want people who have done a lot, so I look for people who have tried to diversify their background, lateral around, get more experience. You don't have to be the smartest person, but if you've experienced something before and you see that situation staring you in the face again, and you've successfully come through once before, you can apply that wisdom, which in many cases beats out pure IQ. And by the way, if you've got good candidates coming in the door, I always feel more pressure as the interviewer. If you've got somebody really good sitting in front of you, that level of talent is a rare commodity, and they are not trying to convince you to hire them; you're trying to convince them to come and work for you.

The truth is, this person is interviewing you just as much as you're interviewing them."

Talent Development and Retention

"What I tell my folks is if you're not interviewing outside this group and outside this company at least once a year, you're doing yourself a disservice. My philosophy on this is: as a leader, it's my job to make sure that people are given the opportunity to learn and grow into their positions, and once they've learned everything they can learn from that position, such that the only challenge is an issue that faces you that day, and the institutional part of the learning is over, they really ought to be looking to me to say, 'What's my next opportunity?' Because opportunity has never lined up with ability, it's never worked out that way. Everybody thinks they're ready for a new job before it comes to them most of the time, so I tell people . . . go interview, because one of two things is going to happen. You're either going to figure out that you've learned what you can learn in this job and you're going to be more rewarded with another opportunity, or you're going to go out there and realize that you've got a pretty good gig and you'll come back reenergized."

Creating a Culture That Supports Talent

"The day you go from being an individual contributor to having people work for you, those people become the primary responsibility of your job. Your paycheck is tied directly to their performance. I have a title that says I'm in charge of marketing and public relations and investor relations, but I really view my job as how I get all of these people motivated, engaged, and moving toward a common goal.

"What you owe your top performers is intolerance for poor performance. It is very demotivating to have a poor performer on the team carried along, because it destroys the concept of a team working toward a common goal. You owe it to the entire team to constantly be looking at who's doing what, what do they have responsibility for, and are they the best possible person you could have in that role. I am also a huge fan of rotation. I believe that high performers will get very bored very quickly once they learn the job, so moving good people around is important because, number one, it keeps the business moving, and then it also creates this kind of contagious atmosphere where you spread some of these top performers' philosophies around as much as possible.

"Lastly, you have to make it fun. We spend more time at work than we do with our families, so you have to provide an atmosphere where people are enjoying themselves. One thing that isn't done enough anymore is telling people when they do a good job—whether that's recognition to the entire organization or just popping your head in the door and saying, 'I really appreciate all the work you put in on that.' Your people need to know that you value them being there and that what they do is important to the organization. I think too often managers kind of act like parents after a while, where they think their job is to only correct. Your job is also to highlight the good stuff and show people what you want replicated."

Leading Talent

"I appreciate the success I've had in my career, but I don't ever view myself as different from the twenty-two-year-old kid right out of college walking through the door to come in and start working in this group. I don't view myself as better than them; I don't think I'm above doing certain things. It has been a strategy for me to try to keep myself grounded in keeping lines of communication open to all the employees in my group, regardless of what level, because you just learn things when people trust you, but if they don't, you'll never hear. Trust, honesty, and integrity are the most important things to me."

CHAPTER 3

Robust Communication

<small>OPEN, HONEST, FRANK, AND COURAGEOUS, BOTH IN-
SIDE AND OUTSIDE THE ORGANIZATION</small>

If you had asked me ten years ago, "John, what is the number one problem you see in the struggling businesses
you're working with?" I would've said, hands down, "lack of
a clear and well-communicated vision and key strategies." As
you saw in Chapter One, this is still a big problem, but now
the single biggest problem I deal with in client organizations
worldwide is lack of open, honest, robust, and courageous
communication. Robust communication is therefore the
third of the six principles of business success.

Why is this? Well, for starters, communication is incredibly complex. As soon as you get more than three or four people in an organization, the number of possible connections in
the communication web mushrooms, and the likelihood of a
communications breakdown increases exponentially. When
you get forty or fifty people in an organization, the opportunity for miscommunication becomes so overwhelmingly
vast that even the best communicators can struggle. Frankly,

it is amazing to me that anything ever gets communicated well in large companies. In addition, there is another level of complexity because communication breakdowns happen on two distinct levels: organizational and interpersonal. Let's look at these one at a time.

Dysfunctional Organizational Communications

You'd think that after a decade and a half as a business improvement consultant, I would have gotten used to how poor the communications are in some organizations, but it still shocks me. I talk with senior managers who tell me they have no clear idea what the vision or the direction of their company is. I sit in meetings and watch people skirt around important issues, ignore major problems, and avoid any level of confrontation, even if it would be productive. I have interviewed thousands of employees who almost all report that they wish they got more information and better communication from their managers.

Once I was asked to deliver a keynote speech on leadership and building a winning culture to the 600 senior managers in a large organization. Just before it was my turn to talk, the president of the company made a presentation on the findings of the annual internal employee satisfaction survey. The survey had been divided into two groups; group 1 was the six hundred or so senior managers and top C-level leaders and group 2 the nearly eight thousand employees. Group 1, the managers and leaders, scored themselves in the 90th percentile and higher on questions such as "clearly communicates the vision," "gives clear direction," "clearly communicates performance expectations," "shows genuine concern for employees," and "takes time to listen to ideas and concerns of employees." Unfortunately, on the same questions, the employees scored the organization in the 30 to 40 percent range. The managers and leaders thought they were doing a nearly perfect job of communicating to their people, but the employees were not of the same opinion. If I didn't see this sort of thing week in and week out, it would almost be amusing, but when I realize the negative impact this kind of dysfunctional communications has on the thousands of people who work in this organization, there is no humor in it at all.

To solve the problem of poor communication at an organizational level, you must make superb communication a top priority by focusing on it, training heavily in it, measuring it, and rewarding those who do it well. The companies I've worked with that have great communication skills at an organizational level have built a culture that highly valued the following aspects of communication:

■ ■ ■

- *Honesty.* Let me make this awesomely simple: tell the truth—all the time. Honesty is without question the most important element in building an organization with strong communication.
- *Empathy.* It is one thing to be honest; it is another thing to be brutally honest. Tell the truth in a frank and direct, yet respectful and empathetic, way. Shoot straight with people, but don't shoot them between the eyes.
- *Courage.* Organizations with a strong communication culture tell the truth about even the most difficult and challenging subjects. They have the courage to put uncomfortable topics on the table and force a discussion. Rather than

hoping that bad things go away, that someone else will fix it, that the problem will solve itself—they start a dialogue about specifically what it will take to address the problem head on and move forward toward a positive solution. Courageous communication also includes having the nerve and confidence to question authority. In some organizations when the leader chooses a direction, even if it is a poor one, everyone else dutifully falls in behind, but a good communicator has the courage to tell the emperor he has no clothes.

- *Safety*. If you want people to tell the truth about even the most difficult and uncomfortable topics, you have to make it safe for them. I remember a woman who pulled me aside after one of my conflict resolution classes to ask me some advice about communicating a difficult issue to her boss. I suggested she simply tell the truth and be honest about her concerns. The woman looked at me as if I had suddenly grown a second nose in the middle of my forehead and said, "Are you crazy? If I said something like that, my boss would vaporize me on the spot." That is hardly what I would consider a safe environment for open and honest communication.

- *Intellectual rigor*. Although people should be safe, ideas should not be. In an intellectually rigorous culture, theories are tested, hypotheses are challenged, and people welcome, even encourage, critical examination of ideas and information, regardless of the source. A perfect example of a communication culture like this is Microsoft, where aggressively poking and prodding ideas is expected. The goal is for only the strongest ideas to survive.

- *Transparency*. A hallmark of great organizations is that they share as much information with all of their stakeholders as they possibly can. Short of actual salary numbers or highly confidential data, winning organizations foster a free flow of information across all levels of the business.

■ ■ ■

An example will demonstrate what an organization with amazing transparency and superb communication skills looks like. About eight years ago, I was invited to the national sales meeting of a $350 million manufacturing company. I had just completed conducting an advanced customer service workshop when the CEO of the company took the stage to tell the entire sales force about the new compensation system. If you talk about changing the percentages and bonuses that salespeople will receive for what they sell, they can determine precisely the impact that even the most complex compensation system will have on their personal income faster than a supercomputer. About ten minutes into the CEO's explanation of the new compensation package people began to mumble. Because he was paying close attention to his audience, he stopped and said, "I'm getting the feeling you're not too happy about this new compensation structure are you?"—to which the entire crowd replied with a booming, "No!" He stood there dazed for a few seconds and then said, "Wow, we really worked hard on this and thought it was not only fair, but pretty darn generous. Obviously you don't feel the same, so here is what we're going to do. We will cancel the workshops for the rest of the afternoon, and all of you are going to work together to rewrite the plan the way you want it to be." He pointed to the chief financial officer, who was standing in the corner of the room, and went on,

"We'll give you access to all the numbers we used to develop this system. Any other information you need, just ask, and we'll get it for you immediately. By four o'clock today, I would like you to come back to me with a compensation plan that you feel 100 percent comfortable and enthusiastic about, and my promise to you is that I will not change it in any way." He then paused and looked around the room, making eye contact with his salespeople before finishing his comments: "The only thing I ask is that you remember that the rest of the company is paid based on what you sell and how much commission you take. I know you all have a great deal of respect for the folks back in the factory who are building the stuff you're selling and you want to make sure they are treated fairly too. So please just keep them in mind as you decide how to divvy up the money."

For the next three hours, small groups discussed and debated what the new compensation package should look like. The CEO, CFO, and I sat and watched the teams in animated conversations about what they wanted. They pored over numbers, asked for spreadsheets, looked at compensation and bonus levels across the organization, and spoke openly and honestly about what they thought was fair and reasonable for everyone in the company. They then assigned leaders from each group to represent their teams in molding the various suggestions into one cohesive compensation package. At 4:00 P.M. the CEO announced that it was time for them to present the new plan and said, "I want you to know that whatever you have decided will be adopted immediately as our new compensation plan. I completely trust all of you and know you have the best interests of our entire organization at heart, just as I do."

As it turned out, they had made some major adjustments to the compensation scheme: they decided to pay themselves less than the original plan and put more into a bonus pool for the entire organization. If they exceeded the goals set for the sales force, not only would they make more money, but so would everyone else in the organization. It was a winning strategy for everyone.

That is a stunning example of trust, candor, safety, intellectual rigor, and transparency. If you can't imagine something similar ever taking place in your company, this is a particularly important principle for you to work on.

Key Skills for Superior Interpersonal Communications

Unfortunately organizations with excellent communications are far too rare, mostly because the number one factor that drives superior organizational communications is superior interpersonal communication skills. If the people inside the organization lack the skills, tools, and motivation to strive for superb interpersonal communications, there is no way to achieve effective organizational communications. The first is a function of the second. Therefore, the best way I can help you improve your organizational communication levels is to help you improve your own interpersonal communication skills. Luckily, good communication is a skill that can be taught and learned. It takes practice and hard work, but with time, it is possible for people to greatly improve their communication skills, and so improve the effectiveness and overall quality of communications within organizations.

I have been teaching advanced communications classes for more than ten years and could fill a volume on just that topic. Instead, I offer what I feel are the most critically important skills and techniques for being a superb communicator. If you study and work diligently on the key ideas I share in the next few pages, I guarantee that your interpersonal communication effectiveness will improve dramatically.

Body Language

Various research studies show that as much as 93 percent of interpersonal communications is nonverbal. That means that facial expressions, eye contact, posture, and how you place your arms and legs send a much stronger message than the words that come out of your mouth. Yet most people give absolutely no thought whatsoever to how they use body language when communicating.

When you are talking to someone, face the person squarely, keeping an open position, good eye contact, and a pleasant expression. Lean in slightly, nodding and using facial expressions to show that you are listening and interested. If the other person is giving you detailed information, take notes, and from time to time summarize the key points and make sure you understand. Superb communicators are vigilant to the messages they are sending with their body language.

You also want to watch the body language of your counterpart for signs that the person is losing interest, is confused, or is upset, which is demonstrated by lack of eye contact, not facing the speaker squarely with an open stance, checking a watch, or making facial expressions that show discomfort or displeasure. When you see any of these things, you must redouble your efforts to engage the listener and use not only your words but also your body language to convey the strongest possible message of interest and focus.

Four Levels of Listening

Level 1 of the four levels of listening is ignoring the other person—that is, not listening at all.

Level 2 is listening while distracted. This is trying to carry on a conversation while checking e-mail and typing out a message on your CrackBerry. For those of you who think you can multitask this way effectively, you are dead wrong: it does not work. Not only are you likely doing all of the tasks poorly, which means you will probably have to do them over again (not much of a time saver), you are also sending a clear message to anyone who's trying to communicate with you that you are not listening and your e-mail is more important than the other person is—not a particularly effective message!

Level 3 is focused listening. At this level, you are highly attuned to the communications of your counterpart, striving not only to understand the logical and informational aspects of their communication but also the emotional content behind them. You are demonstrating strong body language, focused eye contact, and attentiveness.

Level 4 is deep listening, which is usually achieved only between significant others or family members. At this level you are totally in sync with your counterpart, understanding the communication and deeply connecting emotionally.

In the business world, anyone who can maintain level 3 listening is considered a superior communicator. In fact, most folks struggle mightily just to get above level 2.

The most valuable skill for improving your listening is learning to clear your mind and focus only on the speaker. Most people speak at a rate of roughly eighty to a hundred words per minute, but your brain is capable of handling significantly more information than that, which means all of that extra bandwidth gets clogged up with extraneous thoughts, internal dialogue, forming rebuttals, and senseless mind chatter. To be a great listener, you must clear as much of that noise as possible from your mind and focus your entire attention on hearing the message your counterpart is sending. The best way I know to do this is by repeating in my mind, over and over again, what my counterpart is saying: what key points she is focused on, how she seems to be feeling, what message I think she is trying to deliver. I don't worry about what I'm going to say once she stops talking. I don't try to think of a snappy answer or a great story to top hers. I just repeat her message and key ideas in my head, so that even though she says something only once, I hear it numerous times, allowing me to understand and remember it better. This technique takes a lot of practice, but once you get proficient at quieting your mind and focusing on the speaker, you'll be amazed how much more information you will hear and retain and how being this kind of listener can greatly improve your interpersonal communications and relationships. People love to be listened to.

Sensory Modes

Some people have a preferred way to receive information. For example, those who favor the auditory sensory mode like to talk about things. They want to sit and discuss an issue, chat about ideas, toss around possible solutions. These folks do their best learning when they are listening. Other people favor visual learning and need to see things to understand them. When communicating with someone who has a dominant visual sensory mode, you need to bring charts, graphs, and pictures, because those who understand and remember visually need to see and read information. Finally, those who are more intuitive and kinesthetic learn best through thinking about or working directly with the problem at hand. Those who favor the kinesthetic sensory mode need the opportunity to hold on to, take apart, and get connected with ideas. The most important thing to understand about sensory modes is that although most people are fairly comfortable getting information in any of these modes, some are so deeply entrenched in their specific mode that they actually cannot take in information if it is given to them in the wrong mode for them.

I happen to be a strong visual learner: if I can't see it, it doesn't exist to me. If I'm lost and you tell me the directions of where I need to go, I will forget them before I get out of the parking lot. Draw me a map, though, and I'll remember it for ten years. If you want to communicate effectively with someone like me, you have to find a way to express the ideas and information you want me to remember visually; otherwise, you might as well be talking to me in Urdu. Again, not everybody falls as strongly into a sensory mode as perhaps I do, but if the person you are communicating with does, you must flex your communication style to give information in the way that is most comfortable for him or her.

The best way to determine someone's sensory mode is to ask the person to describe his or her most recent vacation in detail. Auditory people will tell you about the sounds and what they talked about, visual people will describe how it looked and what they saw, and kinesthetic people will share with you how they felt and what emotions were stirred. Try it. You'll have fun listening for the key words and phrases that indicate if the person has a dominant sensory mode.

Logic Versus Emotion

Much like sensory modes, some people rely more heavily on logic and facts when they are communicating, while others prefer emotions and feelings. Have you ever had someone speak to you in a completely logical way about something that was upsetting you? They gave you facts, figures, and data to prove why you shouldn't feel the way you do, but their message was not very comforting, was it? Or maybe you have communicated with someone who is totally emotional. There is no logic at all, only feelings, worries, hurt, or anger—also not an effective way to communicate. The goal for great communicators is to balance the two, giving just enough logical arguments to support their position, while also communicating empathy and understanding for the emotional aspects of the issue. Similar to sensory modes, most people are neither totally logical like Mister Spock nor totally emotional, but if you attempt to communicate ideas using the wrong approach, you will not achieve the maximum level of understanding and connection.

Hot Words

I call any word that is ambiguous or indicates strong emotions a *hot word*. The reason is they should burn your ears when you hear them and make you pay attention. For example, when someone says to you, "That project will cost a ton of money," you should reply with something like, "Could you define what a *ton* is in actual dollars?" What is a ton of money to one person might be only a few hundred pounds of money to someone else. Another example of a hot word might be, "We need to get this done fast." So how fast is fast? Is that in the next hour? By the end of business today? By next Friday? Just what is *fast?*

I learned this idea the hard way. Shortly after getting hired into my first job right out of college, my boss called me into his office and said he needed a report on one of our key projects right away. Like a good little minion, I replied, "No problem, I'll handle it," and spun on my heels to run back to my desk. It was late in the day when he made this request, but I stayed at my desk late into the night compiling information, creating spreadsheets, developing flowcharts, and writing a thorough and well-balanced report. Because I was eager to impress, I went to a copy shop and worked until the wee hours of the morning making color copies and binding my masterpiece into a beautiful executive report. I got to the office early the next morning and placed it in the center of my boss's desk—only to find out he had left the evening before for a week of vacation.

When he returned the following week, he picked up the report and flipped to page three (out of thirty-eight), which had a brief bullet point synopsis of the key findings. He read that one page, ripped it out, and said, "Thanks, John. This is perfect, just what I needed." And he headed off to a meeting.

From that day forward, whenever somebody says, "This is important. I'd like you to write something up on it and get it to me as soon as you can," I reply immediately with: "Could you help me understand exactly what you mean by 'important'? Should this become my top priority? Would you describe for me exactly what you'd like to see in the report? When specifically do you need it in your hands?" So when you hear words like *fast, important, expensive, urgent, critical,* or *catastrophic, upsetting, significant problem, major issue, very concerning, troubling,* your ears should start to burn, and you should immediately clarify the meaning by defining what these terms mean to the person. Helping people be precise in their language to avoid ambiguity will save you a significant amount of time and trouble.

Dealing with Conflict

One of the most serious roadblocks to effective interpersonal communication (and, by default, organizational communications effectiveness) is that most people are terrible at dealing with any kind of difficult or stressful conversation. Whether at work, at home, or just trying to navigate in the world, people are faced with numerous situations that cause conflict, pain, and discomfort. Unfortunately, very few people are trained on how to deal with difficult situations and allow themselves to become frustrated and angry, often leading to highly destructive communication. But just a few key techniques and tools can make a huge difference in your ability to deal with conflict.

To keep it simple, three techniques seem to be the most useful to people who attend my conflict resolution seminars: I call them the five stages of conflict, telling stories, and the gap. Learning and applying these will reduce a significant amount of conflict and stress in your life, and your organization.

The Five Stages of Conflict

Stage 1 is *empathetic listening*. At the first sign of emotional escalation, a great communicator stops, asks questions, and listens
intently. No arguing, no defending, no pointing out mistakes—
just genuine, authentic, empathetic listening. Here is an example of what you might say in the first stage: "I can see that you
are frustrated and upset about the situation, and you have every
right to be. Will you please take a few minutes to tell me about
what you're thinking and feeling? I promise not to interrupt or
say anything. I just want to listen to your side of the story until
you feel I understand your concerns completely." Now how
often in your own life do you get this sort of treatment when
you are feeling angry or upset? Probably not much. So if you
learn to do this one thing—hold back at the beginning of a difficult conversation and simply focus on and listen to the other
person and show your sincere concern, you will already be in
the top 10 percent of effective communicators.

. Stage 2 is *I-statements*. In stage 1, you told your counterpart,
"I want to listen to you and understand you." In stage 2, you say,
"Now that I have listened to you and understand how you see
things, I'd like to tell you what I'm thinking and feeling from
my point of view." The most powerful tool I know to do this
effectively is the I-statement. An I-statement allows the communicator to be assertive without being aggressive. A poor communicator might say something like, "You have a bad attitude,
and you are trying to sabotage this meeting by embarrassing me
and attacking my ideas," whereas an effective communicator
might say something like, "It seems to me that you're not very
enthusiastic about my ideas. I feel that the meeting is getting
pulled off track when you, at least from my point of view, are
saying things that seem as if they are aimed at embarrassing me

and making my suggestions look stupid. That may not be your intention, but it is how it feels to me right now."

In the first example I am basically accusing the other person: you did this, you think this, you are that. I am telling him how he is thinking, how he is feeling, why he is acting the way he is—and few people react positively to being told what is going on in their own head. In addition, it is very easy to argue with this sort of approach. "You did that on purpose" results in a quick reply of, "No I didn't," "Yes you did." You can see how this quickly devolves.

In the second example, I am trying to speak strictly from my point of view, my opinions, and my feelings. Some people will say that the second example sounds wimpy, but nothing could be further from the truth. I am still demanding an explanation for poor behavior, but rather than accuse, I am asking for help to understand why it seems as if the other person is attacking me. The key to I-statements is that they must always describe how you are thinking, how you are feeling, how something affected you—that is, from your point of view. The minute you say, "You did that because . . ." or "I think you're a jerk," your I-statement loses all of its power.

This does not mean you are always correct, but you do always have the right to express your concerns, feelings, and thoughts in an unaggressive, honest, and frank way. When I-statements are done properly, it is impossible for the other person to argue. For example, you might say, "When you said that to me in the meeting, I felt like you were trying to embarrass me." The reply from your counterpart might be, "Well, I wasn't." And then you can say, "I know you might not have tried to do it on purpose, but I did feel embarrassed because of what you said." You can argue about intentions all day long, but there is no arguing with me when I express a feeling that I am experiencing.

This very important fact gets to the heart of why I-statements are so valuable: when you use them, you train people how to treat you. If you allow someone to be aggressive, rude, condescending, or insulting and you do not protest, you are basically saying that this way of treating you is acceptable. I-statements allow you to address the negative behavior in an unthreatening yet direct way. However, it is critical that you deliver these sorts of statements in the appropriate tone of voice, with positive facial expressions and good body language; otherwise, they can be taken as condescending or aggressive on your part—not very helpful. I believe that I-statements are one of the most powerful communications tools available for avoiding conflict.

Stage 3 is *finding common ground*. Basically in this stage, you are in negotiations. Your counterpart wants things one way, you want them another way, and the goal is to find a solution that both of you feel good about. In this stage, you say, "I have listened carefully to your concerns, issues, and feelings, to the point where you feel I understand you pretty well. I have also told you how I feel, what I'm thinking, and what my concerns are, from my point of view. It is clear that we see things differently, so my question is, 'What possible solution can we come up with together that will give both of us a positive outcome and improve the way we work together?' I am confident we can get there, but I need your help to make it happen." I know that as you read that sentence, you were probably thinking, "Nobody talks like that in the real world." Actually, they do, at least the ones who are willing to work hard to be superb communicators.

Stage 4 is *positive redirection*. At this point, you realize that you and the other person do not see eye to eye. You shift your focus from trying to reach mutual agreement to attempting to move the person in the direction you want her to go, without causing any further escalation of the situation. The way to do this is by separating the person from the problem. There is a specific sequence for putting together a positive redirection statement:

1. I have listened to you, and I understand your point of view.

2. I have told you how I feel from my point of view.

3. We cannot agree on a compromise that we are both happy with.

4. You are okay as a person, but your behavior [or performance] is not acceptable.

5. If you do not adjust your behavior [performance], some bad things might happen, and I really do not want them to happen.

6. Would you please voluntarily change your behavior so we can get the outcome I am asking for? That would really mean a lot to me. If you refuse, there will likely be negative ramifications, and I don't want that for you.

Here's what this looks like when you put it all together in an actual conversation:

> Susan, I've listened to you very carefully, and I understand you do not think the Tampa project is a high priority. I've tried to convince you otherwise, but you don't seem to

believe me. You're one of the key people on this project and one of our top team leaders, but if you continue to turn your reports in days or weeks late, there is a good chance we are going to miss the deadline, and everyone on the team will lose their opportunity for a bonus. This situation is causing me a lot of stress, and I want to try to resolve it as quickly as possible. Will you please agree to meet all the future deadlines? It's important to me and everyone else on the team. Can I count on you to do that?

I'm sure that some of you will say, "Wow, that is really wimpy," but I beg to differ. I am making an assertive request, but in a nonaggressive way that gives Susan every opportunity to save face and voluntarily change her behavior. I think this is one of the most effective ways to manage people. It's honest, straightforward, and clear without being oppressive or demanding. However, if Susan refuses to change her behavior and turn her reports in on time, it will be necessary to move to stage 5.

Stage 5 is *no alternative*. At this point you have given up any hope that the person will voluntarily change her attitude or behavior. Now it is time to direct her to meet your demands, and if she does not, there will be severe consequences for noncompliance. In other words, you give Susan no alternative but to do what you tell her to do. It has all the elements from stage 4: I understand you; you understand me; we don't see eye-to-eye on this; I think you're a good person but your behavior is not acceptable; this situation is causing a problem; will you please change your attitude or behavior; if not—and here's where things are different—there will be very serious consequences. In other words stage 5 is basically my way or the highway.

I have taught these five stages to thousands of employees at various companies, and after I finish going through all five stages, I always ask this question: "Which stage do most confrontations start in?" The answer is, almost unanimously, "Stage 5"! The problem is that if you start at stage 5, you have nowhere left to go. You have begun with a direct threat, and once you go there, there's no turning back. So my suggestion to you is to start at stage 1 and move your way up the ladder. It may take a few minutes or a few hours, but I can guarantee that if you begin the argument at stage 5, it is already over before it started.

Telling Stories

I have seen a great deal of pain caused in both people's personal lives and inside organizations when people don't realize that they're just telling a story. As humans we are curious creatures. We want to know what's going on, we want to understand what is happening around us, and we do not like it when we can't fill in the blanks. So when they don't have enough information, most people simply make up a story. This story is not based on facts, information, data, or reality (that would actually be a positive and healthy story). But most people do not tell positive, healthy stories; they tell horror stories, based on fear, innuendo, assumptions, and rumors. What happens next is the most insidious part: a completely fabricated story begins to replace reality, and eventually it becomes fact in the thinker's mind, causing pain, anxiety, and stress. Let me tell you a story about how people tell themselves stories.

Many years ago, I was teaching this idea in a conflict resolution class of senior banking executives, when a woman said, "I know exactly what you're talking about." So I asked her to explain and she responded in this way:

> I live on the top of a small hill, and down at the bottom of the hill is my neighbor who rebuilds antique trucks. One day I walked out back and noticed my six-year-old son playing with his dump trucks in the dirt right at the edge of the hill, and I said to him, "Get away from the edge of that hill. You are a clumsy boy, and you're going to trip and roll down the hill right into one of those trucks and knock it off the blocks, and it will land on you and crush your legs. Then I'll run down there and try to lift the truck off the top of you and hurt my back and fall down next to you, and they'll come in an ambulance and take both of us to the hospital, where they'll cut off your legs and I'll have to push you around in a wheelchair for the rest of your life. Now you get away from the edge of that hill before you hurt yourself."
>
> As I finished telling my son this, he looked up at me and said, "Mom, you're sick." And he took his trucks and went to play on the other side of the yard.
>
> But that's just like me. I'm always making up a story. I do it at home, I do it at work, I do it with my family. I do it all the time.

The truth is many of us do. This is why having a well-communicated vision and transparency throughout an organization is so critical. Where there is a lack of information and people don't know or are unsure, they will make up a story. And most often, it will not be a happy, positive, motivating story. Losing a big project becomes a story about looming layoffs. Strange guests touring the factory becomes a story about an impending merger. Rejection of a request to buy new piece of equipment becomes a story about the division being closed down.

The solution for stopping storytelling is twofold. First, realize when you or someone else in the organization is telling a story. Stop yourself before you get caught up in gloom and doom based on assumptions, guesses, and fears. Go get the facts, ask questions, and point out to others that they are not basing their concerns and anxiety on solid information and real data. Second, share as much information as you possibly can with everyone around you. Where there is an abundance of open, honest, and transparent communication, there is little room for silly stories.

Actually it has always been my position that if you're going to make up a story, it might as well be a positive one. If you're going to lie to yourself, why not tell a happy lie? In fact, this is really one of the key roles of effective leader: creating and sharing positive and uplifting stories about the future and collecting real stories that support and exemplify the mission, vision, and values of the organization. A company that does this extremely well is the Ritz Carlton, where every day, at every Ritz Carlton property worldwide, every employee attends "line-up," where they review the priorities for the day; revisit the mission, vision, and values of Ritz Carlton; and are treated to a real story about how one of their peers went above and beyond to live the service values of their organization. Is it any wonder that a company that has created such a strong tradition around communicating the vision through positive storytelling has developed such a renowned reputation for excellence? I think not.

The Gap

The idea of the gap is one of the most useful concepts I teach in my classes. Like most other truly profound ideas, it is just common sense—but not common practice. All your life, you will face difficult situations, upsetting information, and uncomfortable confrontations. Some people react emotionally and aggressively when these sorts of things happen to them. They lose control, yell and scream, and become angry, even abusive. Others react in an opposite manner, remaining calm, cool, collected, and focused. The difference between the two types of reactions is in understanding and applying the gap.

Here is the truth:

No one makes you angry. You anger yourself.
No one makes you frustrated. You frustrate yourself.
No one else makes you lose your temper. You allow your temper to take control.
No one else makes you yell or scream. You choose to behave that way.

No matter what happens to you in your life, there is a gap between when it happens and how you choose to react to it. The gap may be just a few milliseconds or a few hours, but there is always a span of time gap where you have the opportunity to take 100 percent accountability for the decisions you make about how you will behave as a result of the situation.

Regardless of what happens to you in life, you always have the ability to choose your response. And it is in that gap—between the negative stimulus and how you choose to respond to it—where all of the power is because this is where you can choose to act like the "ideal you"—not the way you acted in the past, not what you can get away with, not the way your emotions are driving you. What this means is that you must have a very clear idea of exactly what the ideal you looks like long before you get in a trying or stressful situation. To help you get clear on this, let's do an ideal you exercise.

On a separate piece of paper, write down a few key words or bullet points that describe the ideal you. Imagine that you're in a highly stressful situation; some very negative things have happened, and everyone is looking to see how you will react. What would you say and do if you could handle the situation beautifully? How would you interact with those around you? What sort of demeanor would you have? What sort of words would come out of your mouth? What sort of example would you set if you handled even the worst situations elegantly? How does the ideal you behave under even extreme pressure? Keep your description short and concise—just a few key words or phrases to describe the ideal you.

What you have just created is called an *anchor*: a set of words or phrases that you can use to anchor your mind and focus it in the midst of even the most challenging situations. Acting poorly, getting angry, and losing your temper are merely bad habits that you have gotten into, and the formula for changing habits is to replace the old negative ones with new positive ones. At first it will be very difficult to focus on your ideal-you anchor and control your behavior, but with practice and patience, you will realize that more times than not, you are acting in a new and more positive way. In time, you will eventually become your ideal you as long as you remember that no one can make you do anything. You always have 100 percent control over how you choose to react in every situation.

Now rate yourself on a scale of 1 to 10, with 10 being, "I am like this all the time; I am a living example of my ideal-you behavior; I am the Buddha," all the way down to 1, meaning: "This looks nice on paper, but it is not how I act or behave at all." What is your honest score for how well you truly act like the ideal you right now?

Here's why I asked that question, because no matter what score you gave yourself today, it can be a 9 or 10 in the future. This is a learned behavior. Regardless of how you act or behave now, you have the ability to learn to use the gap to control your anger, emotions, and outbursts.

It is also essential to understand that the ability to control your emotions and reactions no matter what is happening around you is essential for long-term career success. Have you ever worked for somebody who did not understand this idea and lost his temper in a meeting, yelled and screamed at coworkers, or threw a fit when something upset him? How did you feel about that person when he was acting that way? How did that sort of behavior affect your impression of him? Would you want to work for a manager or leader who could not control his or her emotions or temper? Of course not. You simply don't respect someone who does not have the ability to stay calm, focused, and centered in times of chaos and stress. To be a truly great interpersonal communicator and an effective leader, you must learn to take 100 percent control of the gap.

SUMMARY OF KEY POINTS

- Lack of open, honest, frank, and courageous communications is the number one cause of problems in most businesses today.

- Communication effectiveness falls apart on two levels: poor communications at the organizational level, which is driven by poor communication skills at the interpersonal level.

- Managers and leaders often feel they are much better at communicating than their subordinates feel they are.

- Companies that communicate superbly focus on honesty, candor, courage, safety, intellectual rigor, and transparency.

- The key skills for superior interpersonal communications are effective use of body language, focused listening, expert questioning, flexing to sensory modes, providing both logical and emotional arguments, and listening for ambiguous or emotionally loaded hot words.

- One of the most serious blocks to effective organizational communication is the inability of people throughout the company to deal with difficult, stressful, or confrontational conversations.

- There are five stages for handling a confrontation: empathetic listening, I-statements, finding common ground, positive redirection, and no alternative.

- One of the best ways to avoid rumor-mongering, fear, and anxiety in an organization is to help people realize when they are just "telling a story."

- The number one way to avoid losing your temper and communicating in destructive ways is to use the gap and move toward behaving and communicating like the ideal you.

- The key to improving organizational communication is to work on improving your own interpersonal communication skills and then model positive communication skills and behaviors for others in the company to learn from.

EFFECTIVENESS AUDITS

These two brief audits will help you determine how well your organization is doing on the key items outlined in this chapter. It is essential that you be completely honest in scoring the questions. This is not an exercise to get the highest score; it is a diagnostic tool to discover areas that need focus and improvement. On a scale of 1 to 10, with 1 being strongly disagree and 10 being strongly agree, score the following statements.

ORGANIZATIONAL COMMUNICATIONS EFFECTIVENESS AUDIT

1. We have a high degree of open, honest communication throughout our entire organization. _____

2. People in our organization talk in a straightforward and direct way, telling the truth with candor. _____

3. People in our organization are courageous in their communications and not afraid to put even the most uncomfortable or awkward information out on the table for discussion._____

4. The communications environment in our organization is very safe. Anyone can bring up any issue or discuss any topic without fear of reprisal or retribution. _____

5. We have an intellectually rigorous communication style where people are encouraged to openly question and challenge ideas._____

6. Regardless of how much we might challenge or question ideas, our communications always remain completely respectful of the individual who brought the information to the table. _____

7. There is a high degree of transparency throughout our organization._____

8. Critical business information is shared freely throughout the company._____

1. I attend very closely to the body language signals I send when communicating with others. _____

2. When communicating with others, I watch their body language very closely for signals of interest, attention, and understanding. _____

3. I am a highly attentive listener and focus deeply on not only what my counterpart is saying, but also any emotions behind the words. _____

4. I am careful to look for cues indicating my counterpart's preferred sensory mode of receiving information and then flex my style to deliver my communications in the way that is most comfortable for that person._____

5. I am adept at using both logic and emotion to express my ideas and connect with my counterpart._____

6. I listen carefully for ambiguous words or words that I do not understand and then politely ask my counterpart to more clearly define what he or she is trying to express to me. _____

7. I listen carefully for emotionally charged words that indicate anger, confusion, frustration, or disapproval and then politely ask my counterpart to help me understand what he or she is trying to express to me. _____

8. I am skilled at effectively handling difficult or confrontational conversations. _____

9. I am skilled at focusing on facts and real information and seldom allow myself to tell upsetting or stressful stories about situations I do not yet fully understand._____

10. I am skilled at remaining calm, composed, and focused in even the most difficult and challenging situations. _____

EFFECTIVENESS AUDIT SCORING KEY

- A score of 9 or 10 indicates strength in your organization.

- A score of 7 or 8 is a good score but has room for improvement.

- A score of 5 or 6 is an area of concern. This score needs to be brought up because if it heads in the other direction, it could lead to serious issues.

- A score of 3 or 4 is in the danger zone and requires attention and resources to get it moving up the scale quickly.

- A score of 1 or 2 is an emergency and should be dealt with immediately.

THINGS TO THINK ABOUT AND DISCUSS

It is important to take time and give the following questions some serious thought. Be honest with yourself, and think your answers through in detail. You might also find it valuable to gather several people from your organization to discuss these questions as a group, exploring how each of you might answer the same questions differently. These opposing points of view and alternative ideas are critical to developing quality answers.

1. How is the current level of organizational communications affecting your business? Is it helping or hurting your company's performance?

2. In what areas of your organization do you need more transparency and information sharing?

3. Describe how people are treated when they deliver negative or uncomfortable news. Is that productive? What are the ramifications?

4. Describe how people in your organization deal with conflict. Is that productive? What are the ramifications?

5. How well do you communicate with outside stakeholders: customers, shareholders, vendors, suppliers, and partners? Is that productive? What are the ramifications?

TURNING IDEAS INTO ACTION

Here are several suggestions on how you can take some of the main ideas of this chapter and begin to implement them immediately. Some of them might work perfectly for you; others will need some adjustment and customization. Read them carefully, and start thinking about how you can make them work in your organization.

1. Invest in advanced interpersonal communications skills training for key managers and leaders in your organization.

2. Create a lending library of books and training DVDs on communication skills for all employees to access.

3. Use articles and white papers to introduce ideas and topics into the conversation within your organization. In this way, if people are uncomfortable with the ideas presented, they can attack the article instead of each other, but at least the topic is out and being talked about.

4. Pick one critically important issue that is currently undiscussable, and find the courage to put it on the agenda for your next meeting.

5. When someone in the organization delivers uncomfortable or negative news to you, respond with something like, "Thank you very, very much for bringing this to my attention. It is important that I know about information like this as fast as possible. I am very unhappy to hear about the situation, but I am extremely pleased that you felt comfortable to come and tell me about it." In this way you shift from fixing blame to fixing the problem.

6. Establish a written set of communications ground rules that can be used to facilitate more open, honest, and frank discussions. Here is an example of what a set of ground rules might look like:
   - Honesty is the best policy. Always tell the truth.
   - Honesty=safety. The truth will not hurt you.
   - Be tough on ideas but not on people. No personal attacks—ever.
   - It is your job to ask questions and challenge assumptions.

- Don't beat around the bush. Communicate in a straightforward yet respectful way.
- Keep it short and simple. Stay on topic, and follow the agenda.
- Strive for transparency. Share as much information as you possibly can.
- If you have a concern or question, make it known.
- We are all on the same team. The goal is for only the best ideas to survive.

CASE STUDY: INTERVIEW WITH JACK MALCOLM ON EXPERT QUESTIONING

Great communications is not about talking; it is about asking superb questions and listening. I asked one of my good friends, Jack Malcolm, president of the Falcon Performance Group, the most talented and skilled executive trainer I have ever met, to offer his advice for this book. For almost twenty years, Jack has traveled the globe teaching consultative sales, interpersonal communications, and executive-level presentation skills workshops at some of the world's leading companies. Here are some excerpts from my interview with Jack.

■ ■ ■

Why do people need to ask better questions?

"There are three main reasons: questions foster better relationships, they make you more persuasive, and they help you develop your people.

"First, the simple fact is that people like to talk about themselves, and they appreciate others who let them do so. After all, do people with children prefer to talk about their own kids, or listen to other parents talk about theirs? If you want to be liked and trusted by others, get them to talk about themselves, their projects, their business, their interests, their priorities. Questions get people to open up and share their ideas, which helps the entire organization benefit from a more collaborative culture.

"Second, the best way to persuade others is to use questions to help them persuade themselves. People value their own opinion above all others, so it's much more efficient, and longer lasting, to wield influence and sell your ideas by making it their idea, and that can only be done through effective questioning. If you want people who are committed to their work, what better way than to have them motivate and focus themselves than through answering your superb questions?

"Third, how will your people grow in knowledge, ability, and confidence if you give them all the answers rather than asking them questions so they can arrive at the answers themselves? Smart people thrive on working out problems, finding solutions, and answering challenging questions. Particularly in customer service situations, the whole company benefits when people are confident to make the right decisions on the spot."

Why do people have poor questioning skills, and what is the negative impact of those skills on an organization?

"The principal reason that people have poor questioning skills is that they are too focused on themselves—on what they want to achieve out of an interchange with another person. Most of us naturally view the world from the inside out—that is, we think primarily about what we want, our own needs and issues. Ironically, the best way to get what you want is to think outside in. Look at your situation from the point of view of the other person. What are your counterpart's wants, needs, and issues? Asking questions shows an interest in another person, and that is one of the quickest ways to build trust. Talking too much typically indicates arrogance and destroys trust. Do I need to ask which way you prefer to be viewed?

"I've also seen that poor questioning practices by managers can make their subordinates feel pressured. For example, in my work with sales teams, I've seen business reviews where the questions seemed to be aimed at 'gotchas' rather than true understanding of the situation. The result: people will tell management what they think is in their own best interest or will be afraid to tell them bad news. That's one reason that high-level managers are often the last to know what's really going on until it's too late. I also think that although questioning has always been important, in today's multicultural business environment, with people from every imaginable background, the ability to ask thoughtful questions is more critical than ever in helping you to clarify meaning and prevent misunderstandings.

"Finally, if you are doing a good job in finding the best people to work in your organization, it would be senseless not to tap into their knowledge, experience, and insight. If you think that your role as a leader means having the right answers instead of the right questions, you will waste the value of your most important asset: the brains of your people."

What are the absolute top questioning skills—the ones that will have the most positive impact right away?

"The first skill is not a skill at all. It's simply an attitude that I call the 51+ rule: take at least 51 percent of the responsibility for the transfer of meaning in each aspect of communication. When you tell someone something, don't assume they understood it exactly as you intended. Question them to make sure. When someone tells you something, clarify his or her meaning. Make sure you're both talking about the same thing.

"Know what you are looking for. If you take a few minutes to think carefully about what you want to know or to accomplish with your questions, you'll sound a lot more intelligent and save a lot of time for all concerned.

"Provide context. If you have a lot of questions, let the other person know why you are asking. It will make them more receptive to your questions and can usually save you a lot of time. For example, you might say there are several ways to approach the issue. If I can ask a couple of questions, we can both make sure we're working on the best solution.

"Know when to zoom in and out. There's a common misconception that questions are only closed-ended and open-ended, and that open-ended questions are better for getting people to give you a lot of information. In reality, open-ended questions asked too early, especially about emotional topics, can actually close down communication. In those cases, it's best to ask questions that are easy to answer and then probe to dig deeper as necessary. For example, instead of saying, 'What's wrong?' you may begin with, 'Are you having a rough day?' and then probe further from there.

"Know how to ask 'nonquestions'—how to get information without making it an interrogation. This may sound contradictory to what I've already said, but too many questions can turn somebody off. You can get the response you want without a question mark at the end of your statement. For example, you can say, 'That must cause problems for you,' or, 'Hmm, tell me more about that,' or 'Help me understand.'

"Be careful you don't ask questions that close out other answers. This is especially important for managers. Sometimes we ask leading questions to confirm our own beliefs. Our subordinates are not stupid; they can sometimes sense what you want the answer to be by how you phrase the question. The classic example is any question that begins, 'Don't you think . . . ?'"

What specifically can people do to improve their questioning skills?
"The most important thing anyone can do to improve their questioning skills is to simply ask more of them. Remind yourself before conversations of the 51+ rule, and then make an effort to get the other person to talk more than you do.

"You can also make it a game. I'm reminded of the basketball movie *Hoosiers,* in which the coach told every player he wanted to see five passes before anyone took a shot. When people ask your opinion, for example, try to ask several questions before firing back with an answer.

"In some cases, such as before important meetings, prepare by writing down a list of questions.

"You can also learn by observing the good questioners in your own organization.

"Finally, depending on your role in the organization, there are some good books available to learn questioning techniques for specialized situations, such as selling, root cause analysis, decision making, solving, and others. If you are serious about improving your questioning skills, it is going to take some serious studying and lots of practice, practice, practice."

CHAPTER 4

Sense of Urgency

A FAST, AGILE, ADAPTABLE ORGANIZATION THAT
MAKES THE IMPORTANT THINGS HAPPEN NOW

Here is another awesomely simple fact: speed equals success. In today's business world, if you can't move fast, you're gone. Hence, a sense of urgency is the next principle of business success. It wasn't all that long ago that getting a message from London to Los Angeles would have taken more than a month; now it's nanoseconds. We learned in business school that competitive differentiation was based on speed, price, or quality: pick two and position yourself in the marketplace. Well, the Internet has completely changed the rules of the game. Now you must deliver very high quality, at the lowest possible price, with superior customer service, and right now! That's right: all four—all the time—for every customer.

Speed rules because customers have zero tolerance for waiting. Expectations are measured in download speed. There was a time when you could tell customers to expect four to six weeks for shipping and delivery. Now if you can't get it there the next day or faster, you don't get the sale. Speed rules because the first one with a successful new product to market now enjoys a smaller and smaller window of opportunity. It used to be that if you came out with a really good product, you had eight months to a year before you'd see a knock-off; now it's down to a few weeks. Speed rules because while you and your team are sitting around trying to make a decision about entering a new market, creating a new partnership, or developing a new distribution channel, your competition has already beaten you there.

I'm not talking about out-of-control, 400-mile-an-hour, hair-on-fire speed. What I am saying is that in most cases (though not all), faster is better than slower when it comes to how your company operates. My experience is that all great organizations run at a fast pace. People throughout the business have a sense of restlessness. They're never satisfied, always striving for improvements, agitated at any delays, intolerant of things that waste time, ready to get going right away. Companies that fail have a mañana attitude. *We'll get to that tomorrow,* they say. *There's no rush; they can wait.* The truth is "they" can't wait, and they won't. Agility, speed, flexibility, anticipation, adaptability, and a strong sense of urgency throughout the organization are required for survival in business today regardless of the size of your business.

So if you agree that a quick pace really matters, how then do you create an organizational culture that reflects a strong desire to get the most important things done quickly and never waste time on the trivial? Three key elements combine synergistically to create a company that is light on its feet and ready to move quickly:

Clear direction + free flow of information + fast decision making = An agile organization.

Creating a Clear, Intended Outcome

One of my favorite scenes in *Alice in Wonderland* is when Alice comes to the fork in the road and asks the smiling Cheshire Cat which road she should take. The cat says to Alice, "That depends a good deal on where you want to get to," to which Alice says, "Oh, it really doesn't matter." That cat's famous reply is, "Then it doesn't matter which way you go."

Because I have seen so many businesses that operate exactly this way, some of my consulting colleagues and I developed a small mathematical equation to describe this conundrum:

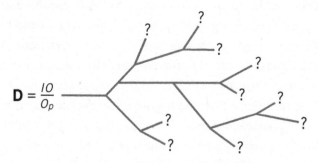

$$D = \frac{IO}{Op}$$

What this impressive little equation stands for is: decisions *(D)* equal intended outcome *(IO)* over number of options *(Op)*. Now before you try to plug in numbers and see if it works, it doesn't. We made this up one afternoon while drinking beer at a barbecue restaurant and lamenting the fact that so many of our clients had no clear intended outcome for their businesses. This lack of direction caused them to get totally bogged down in trying to make even the simplest strategic decisions, which eventually led to their calling us for help. Although some consultants say, "If you can't fix the problem, there's good money to be made in perpetuating it," I'm in the camp that believes we are there to give sound guidance, solid information, and as much help as possible, so we developed this equation to demonstrate to our clients why having a clear, intended outcome is so vitally important. Instead of trying to explain the concept behind the equation in business terms, let me give you a different type of example that I hope will make it clear.

Let's say I am staying at a hotel in downtown Manhattan and go to the concierge and say, "I'm really hungry and would like to go out for dinner. Can you recommend someplace, please?" Without any additional information from me (in other words, no clear "intended outcome" for the dining experience I am trying to achieve), the concierge would have a hard time making an absolutely perfect restaurant suggestion. At last count, there were more than nine thousand restaurants in the greater New York metropolitan area. How easy is it to make a fast and high-quality decision with nine thousand possible options? The answer is that you can't.

Now let's say I give the concierge a clear intended outcome, for example: "I would like to go to a sushi restaurant for dinner this evening, preferably one that does not play that loud, clanging kabuki music because I want to relax and read a book during dinner. I don't really want to take a cab, so I'd like to go to someplace close enough that I can comfortably walk to it, let's say ten to fifteen blocks. Also, I don't want to have to wait more than twenty minutes to get seated, and I would like my meal to cost less than eighty dollars." Now we go from nine thousand possible options to probably only two or three that meet these criteria. At that point, the concierge can use his knowledge of the local area and personal experience to recommend the sushi bar that will meet all my needs and deliver a fabulous dining experience within my constraints.

It is the same thing in business. Without a clear, vivid, and detailed vision of the future (intended outcome), people are overwhelmed with a myriad of possible priorities and decisions (options) and are unable to make fast, focused decisions. This is also why it is so critical to overcommunicate the vision. If the vision is written down in a hundred places, painted on banners, and carved in a giant rock in front of the building but it is not a living part of the culture, it is the same as not having one. The more you can help people understand and focus on the intended outcome, the more aggressively and quickly your organization can move toward that outcome:

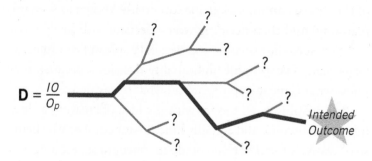

Another important way that having a well-communicated intended outcome helps the organization is by showing people what *not* to do—what projects we won't pursue, what clients we don't want to serve, what markets we don't want to compete in. Several years ago I was preparing to teach a class on strategic thinking at Cornell and had a sudden epiphany that truly good strategic thinkers are not only superb at creating focus on a specific intended outcome, but they are also highly skilled at figuring out what to say no to:

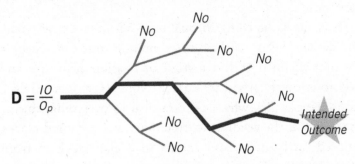

Here is another awesomely simple idea: it is definitely important to have a prioritized to-do list, but it is perhaps more important to also have a prioritized "to stop" list!

All decisions are based on weighing the potential outcomes of the various options available (otherwise known as scenario planning) and then deciding which decision will likely move you closest to the outcome you desire. People in fast organizations make fast yet still high-quality decisions because they know what is most important and what to say no to.

It is possible to go too far with the idea of creating a clear, intended outcome and actually hinder your company by being so obsessively focused that you do not recognize better opportunities or when it is time to change direction. The vast majority of organizations I've worked in needed more focus, not less, but every now and then, it's a good idea to pick your head up from the path and take a look around to make sure you're on the right track. I believe the most famous example of this was the story of Andy Grove and Gordon Moore of Intel when they made the painful decision to get out of memory chips and focus on processors. At the time, Intel was the world's leader in memory chips, but Grove and Moore saw the writing on the wall and took the courageous step of completely abandoning the memory business in favor of a new strategy based on processors. Had they stayed focused on their original intended outcome, it is likely that it would have led to the destruction of the company. But by being highly aware, agile, and adaptable when necessary, they were able to make a major course correction that allowed their company not only to survive but thrive.

Urgency Is Allergic to Bureaucracy

Nothing on the face of the earth is as deadly poisonous to a culture of urgency as bureaucracy. Red tape strangles urgency in a death grip. Multiple layers of decision makers crush initiative under the oppressive weight of indecision. If speed = success, bureaucracy = failure.

To create a culture that allows your top talent to deliver outstanding work with a high sense of urgency requires eliminating every possible impediment to fast action and the free flow of information across every level of the organization. Successful leaders give their people all of the tools, information, and resources they need to excel at their jobs and then get out of their way. To quote my friends at Microsoft, "Stop the insanity." Stop any meeting, discontinue any report, eliminate any procedure, kill any rule, revamp any process that does not add real value to the organization, and allow people to do their jobs more efficiently, effectively, and quickly.

Imagine if a major organization were to take a handful of their most talented people—a key marketing manager, the lead information technology project manager, the national sales director, a few top engineers, a regional product manager, and a senior customer support manager—and put them all in a room for a typical four-hour corporate meeting; they would be tying up hundreds of thousands, if not millions, of dollars of time, talent, and salary in what will most often turn out to be an utterly useless meeting. Would you knowingly throw that kind of money away? Of course not; no sane leader would. But they do it every day. In a situation like that, the rule should be that if you are not getting hundreds of thousands or millions of dollars of value from putting these people in this meeting, cancel it. Or at least cut the meeting length in half. Or let people leave the meeting as soon as their part is done. Or teleconference a few of them in for only the parts they need to participate in. Do whatever it takes to get people out of senseless meetings so they can do the real work of making critical decisions and moving the business ahead quickly.

A few years ago I worked with a Fortune 100 company in which almost every manager I knew had thirty or forty hours of meetings planned per week in addition to their regular work. That is complete lunacy, and everyone in the organization knew it. They sat in meetings on their Black-Berries, listened in on phone conferences while trying to get e-mails done and type reports, and spent half a day in a meeting to give a ten-minute presentation. Hours and hours every single week, hundreds and hundreds of talented people wasted their time and the company's money. Here is what happened to that company: all of the really smart people who could not stand the frustration of endless stupid meetings quit and went to the competition. The flow of quality information came to a halt, the speed of decisions fell to just below glacial, and this multibillion dollar company no longer exists. True story.

I am in no way saying that meetings are not important. Indeed, they are critical to business success, but only as long as they are well run, focused, highly productive meetings that stay on agenda and on time and result in sound decisions, specific actions, and clear accountability. How many meetings like that do you attend a year?

Topple the Pyramid

The only thing that can slow you down more than bureaucracy is senseless layers of hierarchy. A leader's job is to break down barriers, not build up monuments to his or her own importance. I have worked in ten-person organizations with an unbelievable four layers of hierarchy.

Organizations that embrace a sense of urgency make it easy for people to navigate the structure of the business. Transparency, open-door policies, skip-level meetings, and access to even the highest-level executives are the norm in all of the successful organizations I have worked in. Nearly every company understands that in today's business culture, the old command-and-control, organization-chart-driven hierarchy of the past is dead. So the question is: Have you killed all senseless hierarchy in your company so that your people can spend time doing work and meeting with customers, not navigating the red tape and playing politics?

Four-Level Decision Making

I learned early in my career that the only way to keep a company moving forward quickly is to give people as much independent decision-making authority as possible. If every decision has to come across your desk, pretty soon the entire organization will come to a grinding halt. However, most employees are really good at reverse-delegating. You assign them a project, and tell them to handle it, and they keep wandering back into your office asking for direction. In a culture that embraces a strong sense of urgency, decisions need to be made at the lowest level possible, with the fewest number of people involved. As a young leader, I thought it was really cool to make all of the decisions because it felt like my people needed me—until I became overwhelmed by the steady stream of people standing at my desk and asking for a decision. It was good for my ego but terrible for the business, so I developed a system I call *four-level decision making* to delegate decisions effectively across the organization. From that point forward, whenever I managed a team or an entire company, I used this system:

■ ■ ■

- *A level 1 decision is one that you own completely as the employee.* You should be totally comfortable making this decision, quickly and confidently, without any input from others. This decision is right in your area of expertise, so I expect you to handle it. *Example:* If a cashier accepts a personal check from a customer, there is no reason that a manager needs to come over and look at the check too. This oversight adds absolutely no value to the equation.

- *A level 2 decision is one in which you get some advice from the appropriate person in the organization.* After you have consulted one or possibly two people, go ahead and make a level 2 decision and own it. *Example:* A marketing manager asks members of the sales team for their thoughts on a new advertising concept. The marketing manager needs to make the decision herself, but getting the thoughts from the people who are selling the product is a good idea.

- *A level 3 decision is a team decision.* We will get all of the appropriate people together, discuss and debate, and whatever the team decides, I will go along with, even if I do not agree. I trust the team to make this decision together, but as the leader, I own the responsibility if something goes wrong. *Example:* We need to decide whether to move the company into a new market or stay focused in the current market and instead try to increase market share. This decision affects nearly everyone in the organization, so involving representatives of various departments in the decision is a good idea. We gain the wisdom of their experience and their commitment to the implementation of the decision.

- *A level 4 decision is my decision.* I ask for thoughts and advice from various members of the team, possibly the entire team, but in the end I am going to make this decision on my own, and I will own the outcome. On a level 4 decision, you have to trust that I'm doing what's in the best interests of everyone on the team. *Examples:* Creating high-level strategic alliances, selling off part of the business, buying another company, terminating a major project, or investing significant money in a new project are all decisions that a leader wants to get lots of input on, but in the end, he or she is the one to put a stake in the ground and say, "This is my decision."

■ ■ ■

After I had made the four levels of decisions clear to everyone, I would get in the habit of pointing out which level decision a person was faced with. Someone would walk into my office and start to explain a problem, and I'd say, "Whoa, stop right there. That's a level 1 decision. You need to handle that one completely on your own." Or I might say, "That's a level 2 decision. You need some input on that, but I'm not the best person to give it to you. Go down and talk to Jim [the CFO] and ask him about the numbers. Then you make this decision based on your best judgment."

Rarely did we ever come across level 3 decisions, and even rarer were level 4. What eventually happened was that people learned the different types of decisions, and took responsibility for handling the levels 1 and 2 decisions without ever involving me. The outcome was much faster and usually much better decisions by employees who felt empowered and responsible for guiding the direction of the company. This sort of decision-making process is critical to creating a culture of urgency.

When You Do Have to Make a Level 3 Decision

From time to time, it is necessary to bring together an entire team of people to make a decision. This can be a treacherous situation, fraught with opportunities to see a group of bright people take far too long to make a really poor decision. Although it is wonderful to have the benefit of the experiences and ideas of a wide array of people, the goal in a culture of urgency is speed while still delivering the best possible decision. I have watched this process unfold both beautifully and painfully in organizations around the world. In the companies that were able to achieve consensus quickly on high-quality decisions, there seemed to be a pattern of key questions they asked themselves as they went through the decision-making process. Here is my take on a framework for improving your group decision making. (I am assuming that you have already correctly identified that the situation truly requires a level 3 team-based decision.)

■ ■ ■

1. *In/out: Do I really add value to this decision-making process? Should I even be involved in this decision?* There is no reason to have ten people involved in the decision when only six of them have the knowledge, authority, and ability needed for the decision. Every additional person involved in making the decision will multiply the difficulty and complexity of the decision, so keep the number of decision makers to the absolute minimum required to get the best decision.

2. *Go/no go: Do we have the right people present and all of the information we need right in front of us to make the decision at this time?* There is no point in laying out all of the information and data if you don't have all of the people who need to be involved in the decision present. On the flip side, there is no reason to bring the team together to make a decision if you

do not have all the information they will need in hand. Having the entire decision-making team sitting around waiting for one last person to arrive or someone to finish a report is a waste of time. Have everyone go back to work until you're ready to sit down and make the decision together.

3. *Timing: When do we really need to have an answer?* One of the most common mistakes is to rush a decision that did not need to be made right away or take so long to make a decision that the marketplace or the competition makes it for you. Yes, speed rules, but that doesn't mean that every decision is life and death and must be made immediately. Take a minute to determine the real amount of time you have to make the decision, and then take as long as is necessary to make a quality decision—and not one second longer.

4. *Viable options: What are the three or four real options we have on the table?* There are two major mistakes this question is trying to help you avoid. The first is getting caught up in the brainstorming trap that there's no such thing as a bad idea and generating so many outlandish and unrealistic options (along with a few good ones) that it is overwhelming to choose among them. The second track is the opposite: choosing the first right answer that comes to mind. All our lives, throughout school and college, we are taught to find the "one right answer," and that's a hard habit to break. But the truth is, especially in making decisions, there can often be several right answers, and you want to make sure that each of them sees the light of day for discussion and debate.

5. *Probability and impact: If we make a certain decision, what is the probability it will go wrong, and what would the impact be if it did?* This is a quick-and-dirty risk analysis. If it is low probability and low impact, you can make the decision quickly.

If it is high probability and high impact, it is time to stretch out the decision as long as you possibly can to collect as much information, data, input, and advice as can be obtained. An example from my personal background explains this well. I grew up in south Florida, right in the middle of hurricane alley. If a storm formed in the deep South Atlantic and was moving slowly northward at a category 1 level, that was low probability and low impact and did not require any action. However, if the storm was crossing Havana at a category 4 level and headed straight for Miami, it was time to get out of town. Consider this, though: if the director of the storm center, who was charged with making the decision to evacuate part of the state, decided to tell people to get out of town, this was a high-impact, high-probability multibillion-dollar decision. Another area to look at is low probability but extremely high impact. Examples are the *Challenger* and *Columbia* disasters, Chernobyl, or a major earthquake hitting Los Angeles. These are the sort of situations where you need to listen to the dissenters on your team and foster disagreement so that the team does not get too anchored on the opinions of the more influential members. The loudest or most confident are not always the most accurate. On risky decisions, it is important to build out several different scenarios with varying degrees of probability and impact and be sure to have among them (even as outlandish as they might seem) remote possibilities that could prove disastrous. If you decide to be bold and bet that you can beat the odds, make sure you can survive if the odds beat you.

6. *Ripple effect: Who else will be affected by the decision we make?* In my example about the storm center, the ripple effect of making the evacuation decision is monumental. I know most decisions are not on that scale, but many decision

makers fail to take even a few minutes to think through the ripple effect of the decision they are about to make.

7. *Make the decision: Based on everything we know now, what is the best possible decision that we can make?* If you have done the previous six steps diligently and answered the questions honestly, now it is time to gather the team and make the decision. The key point here is that we're not going for 100 percent agreement; we are going for consensus. What consensus means to me is this: "Unless I feel absolutely opposed, as a member of the team I am willing to trust the rest of my team and go along with their decision if it is different from mine. Furthermore, once I cast my vote with the rest of the team in consensus or even abstain but agree to go along with the consensus, it is absolutely critical that I support the team decision unwaveringly to the rest of the organization." There is nothing worse than a team that fights through a difficult decision to arrive at hard-won consensus, only to have one of the team members leave the meeting and bad-mouth the decision to everyone else in the organization. That sort of behavior is unacceptable and should be dealt with in the strongest terms.

A lot of people stop the meeting right here. They think, "I got together with my team, we yelled and screamed, we threw stuff around the room and we came up with what we think was the best possible decision. Time to go to happy hour." Not so fast. A decision is not a decision until a clear plan for implementation has been developed and a single individual has been assigned the responsibility for implementation. We delve into this in much more detail in the next chapter, but there are at least two more steps to the decision-making process.

8. *Implementation: What are the specific action steps that must take place to implement this decision, and who will be responsible for making sure they are accomplished?*

9. *Follow-up: What is the specific time line of key deliverables, and who will monitor progress to hold the team "action owner" accountable?*

■ ■ ■

I'm not saying to do all nine steps for every decision, but for any major decision—any high-probability, high-impact decision—I strongly urge following this process to the letter. In all the years I have been coaching and consulting businesses, I can count on one hand the number of organizations I've worked with that were truly effective in making critical decisions. Most skip steps, rush decisions, make incredibly important decisions based on assumptions and flimsy data, neglect to give any consideration to the ripple effect, and completely ignore implementation or follow-up. The list of disasters is long and the financial implications devastating (just look at the total debacle on Wall Street, the mortgage industry, the banking industry, the insurance industry, and the auto industry in late 2008), and you don't want to be on it.

Reward Fast Action

You don't always get what you ask for from employees, but you almost certainly get what you reward for. To create a culture of urgency requires building both formal and informal systems for celebrating people who take initiative and make things happen. When people throughout the organization see that agility, accountability, looking for responsibilities, and taking action are highly valued and rewarded, you will see a change in attitude. However, there are two caveats to this recommendation. First, if you ask people to move quickly and make decisions with speed, they are going to make mistakes from time to time. Tolerance for prudent risk taking and acceptable business failures goes hand-in-hand with a culture that encourages a sense of urgency. People need to know that it's absolutely safe to make a mistake, as long as it was in an effort to make the right things happen quickly. Second, people who do not move quickly or who tie everything up in politics and personality must be dealt with decisively. There is nothing more frustrating to top performers than pushing them to embrace a sense of urgency, only to allow them to run into a brick wall of bureaucracy.

I go into much more depth on rewards, celebrations, and praise in the next chapter, but the important point is that people are motivated for their own reasons, not yours. In order for a reward to motivate someone, it has to be valuable to him or her personally. For some people, that might be money, for others public recognition, for others a day off. But if you give someone the wrong kind of reward—for example, public recognition in front of the entire company to someone who is painfully shy—you've just ensured that this person will never, ever repeat those results again. Motivation = *motive for action,* and it is unique for every person, just as the reward should be.

Multiply the Speed of Your Brain

I'm now going to share with you one of the most important ideas in this book. Actually it's the most important thing I've ever learned in my life so far. That's a pretty big claim to make, but here it is: *You become what you focus on and become like the people you spend time with.*

Whatever you think about, whatever you fill your mind with, whatever you focus on, and whomever you choose to surround yourself with will in large part determine what your life will look like a decade from now. This is true at both the personal and organizational levels. From a business point of view, it is my contention that if you focus intently on the six principles I have laid out in this book, you are spending your time and energy on the key elements to make your business successful. The next step is to surround yourself with a broad network of bright, talented people who want to see you succeed. On one level, this is the talent you bring into your organization—the stellar employees you attract to your team. Just as important is a second level of people who want to help and support you: a vast network of colleagues, mentors, and associates who are actively involved in helping you create a truly great organization. The reason this is so critical is that in today's business world, nobody has all of the answers. You can't make it alone; you need help. We all do. So it is imperative that you surround yourself with smart people and ask them for as much help as they are willing to give you.

Several years ago, I received an unexpected call from the CEO of one of my top client firms. "John," he said, "I have a corporate espionage emergency. We've just discovered that two of our vice presidents have been stealing files and are trying to set up another business to compete directly with ours. I've never faced this before, and I need your help. What should I do?" I explained that I was away from my office at that moment, but would go back immediately and send him a memo with my very best advice by the end of business that day. I then hung up the phone and gathered my thoughts. I knew absolutely NOTHING about corporate espionage and had never dealt with it before in my career. So I rushed back to my desk and typed out an e-mail to a few dozen of my top-level contacts at a number of major corporations. Within minutes of hitting Send on my keypad, the phone started to ring. Within a few hours, I had received calls and e-mails from nearly two dozen senior executives who had all dealt with corporate espionage in their careers and were eager to offer their advice and guidance. I took all of the advice these talented people gave me and wrote a memo to my client, letting him know that these were not just my ideas but also the ideas I had garnered from my network of top-level executives.

Two weeks later, I received a call from my client. He told me, "We hired one of the top corporate espionage attorneys in the country to help us with this case, and when he arrived, we showed him the memo you sent to us. He said it was the single finest memo on what to do if faced with corporate espionage that he had ever seen and asked for a copy of it. John, we can't possibly thank you enough for your help and guidance in the middle of this terribly difficult situation."

Here's the point. At 9:00 on the morning of that first call from the CEO, I knew nothing about corporate espionage, but by 4:00 P.M., I was able to deliver highly valuable information and advice to assist my client in making a fast and high-quality decision. It should be no different for you. If you surround yourself with a huge network of extremely talented people, both inside and outside your organization, and get in the habit of asking for help, you'll soon realize that you can gather the information, experience, ideas, and information you need to support an organization with a strong sense of urgency and a bias for action.

SUMMARY OF KEY POINTS

- Speed = success. You must create a culture of urgency.

- Clear direction + strong information flow + fast decision making = an agile organization.

- You can't make fast decisions if you don't know where you're going.

- $D = IO/Op$. Decisions equal intended outcome over number of options.

- A major part of strategy is figuring out what to say no to.

- If speed = success, then bureaucracy = failure.

- Be ruthless in eliminating any process, rule, system, procedure, or meeting that does not add real value in helping your people be more effective, efficient, and quick in doing their work in serving customers.

- Topple the pyramid: destroy unnecessary levels of hierarchy.

- Use four-level decision making to empower your people to make fast decisions. To recap: level 1—you own this decision completely on your own; level 2—get some advice from the right people, and then you make the decision and you own it; level 3—we will make this decision as a team; and level 4—as the leader, I'll ask for your advice and input, but I will make this decision on my own and will own it.

- When you have to make a level 3 team decision, use the nine-step decision-making process.

- You don't necessarily get what you ask for; you get what you reward. Reward people for taking fast action.

- You become what you focus on and become like the people you spend time with.

- Multiply the speed of your brain by surrounding yourself with a network of bright, sharp, talented people who want to see you succeed. Then ask them for help and advice often.

EFFECTIVENESS AUDIT

This brief audit will help you determine how well your organization is doing on the key items outlined in this chapter. It is essential that you be completely honest in scoring the questions. This is not an exercise to get the highest score; it is a diagnostic tool to discover areas that need focus and improvement. Score the following statements on a scale of 1 to 10, with 1 being strongly disagree and 10 being strongly agree.

1. People throughout our organization show a strong sense of urgency. _____

2. We have a clear, well-communicated direction that allows people to make decisions quickly on key priorities. _____

3. There is a free flow of information across the organization to help people make good decisions quickly. _____

4. Everyone in our organization understands the top priorities for action. _____

5. Everyone in our organization understands what to say no to. _____ .

6. We have an organization that is superb at focus, discipline, and action. _____

7. There is very little bureaucracy, red tape, or politics in our organization._____

8. There is not a lot of hierarchy or turf guarding within our organization._____

9. Our organization is excellent at making good decisions quickly. _____

10. Our organization has an effective process for making team-based decisions._____

11. When we reach consensus on a team-based decision, we never have problems with people on the team saying negative things about the decision to the rest of the organization._____

12. We support and reward people who have a bias for action. _____

13. We have an organizational culture that makes it safe to take prudent business risks. _____

EFFECTIVENESS AUDIT SCORING KEY
- A score of 9 or 10 indicates strength in your organization.

- A score of 7 or 8 is a good score but has room for improvement.

- A score of 5 or 6 is an area of concern. This score needs to be brought up because if it heads in the other direction, it could lead to serious issues.

- A score of 3 or 4 is in the danger zone and requires attention and resources to get it moving up the scale quickly.

- A score of 1 or 2 is an emergency and should be dealt with immediately.

THINGS TO THINK ABOUT
AND DISCUSS

It is important to take time and give the following questions some serious thought. Be honest with yourself, and think your answers through in detail. You might also find it valuable to gather several people from your organization to discuss these questions as a group, exploring how each of you might answer the same questions differently. These opposing points of view and alternative ideas are critical to developing quality answers.

1. What are five specific things you can do immediately to reduce the bureaucracy in your organization?

2. What are five specific things you can do immediately to reduce the hierarchy in your organization?

3. What steps can you take to roll out four-level decision making across your organization?

4. What are three things your organization can do right away to reward people who are proactive, ask for responsibility, and have a sense of urgency and a bias for action?

5. Who are the individuals who inhibit fast action within your organization? The people who use hierarchy, politics, and red tape to slow down the process? What can you do immediately to deal decisively with these people and encourage them to adopt a sense of urgency and fast action taking?

6. Who can you bring into your informal network, as a mentor, colleague, or advisor, to help you make superb decisions even faster?

TURNING IDEAS INTO ACTION

Here are several suggestions on how you can take some of the main ideas of this chapter and begin to implement them immediately. Some of them might work perfectly for you; others will need some adjustment and customization. Read them carefully, and start thinking about how you can make them work in your organization.

1. Develop multiple ways to encourage, support, and communicate the need for the entire organization to embrace a strong sense of urgency.

2. Clearly communicate the direction and key priorities of the organization so that people understand exactly what they should be focused on.

3. Clearly communicate what is not a priority: clients you don't want to serve, markets you do not want to compete in, and projects that are not a priority, for example. Help people understand what they should say no to and walk away from.

4. Create a document that outlines the nine steps of effective team decision making, and begin using it in every meeting where a team has to make a decision.

5. Establish an advisory panel of customers, colleagues, and talented people in your community to give you advice and guidance.

6. Establish clear and aggressive timetables for accomplishing major priorities to ensure that people understand that fast action is critical to organizational success.

7. Establish a committee to review all current processes, systems, and procedures, and look for ways to reduce bureaucracy, red tape, and anything that inhibits agility and quick decision making.

CASE STUDY: BRINGING A COMPANY BACK FROM THE BRINK

As a serious student of business, I was keeping a close eye on the developments at Xerox as it struggled mightily to avoid bankruptcy in 2000. When Anne Mulcahy took over the reins as CEO, it was, in her own words, not exactly the "dream of a lifetime" to inherit a company with nearly $19 billion in debt and a share price that had been cut in half. Rather than doing what many turnaround CEOs would do (slash, burn, and cut), she decided to make a phone call. Even though she did not know him personally, Mulcahy was able to get Warren Buffett on the phone and eventually join him for dinner to discuss what he recommended as the best course of action for turning around Xerox. His advice was simple but powerful: listen to your customers, and take care of your employees.

Mulcahy followed his advice, but what she heard was not exactly exciting. Customers told her that her company was not responsive enough, analysts told her that the company was not focused enough, and employees simply said that management had not been clear enough about specifically what they needed to do to succeed. Based on this feedback and much more, Mulcahy staged a comeback that by any standards was swift and staggering. Just a few years later, Xerox went from losing $300 million a year to making nearly $1 billion, and Mulcahy was named one of the three most powerful women in the world by *Fortune* magazine. I would summarize the strategy she pursued as based on four key ideas:

1. Surround yourself with a huge network of incredibly talented people who are invested in your success. These are people with complementary skills, diverse opinions, and interesting experiences who want to contribute to your vision.

2. Ask for help. Just because you're the leader doesn't mean that you're supposed to have all the answers. Far from it. Once you gather a large group of talented supporters, go to them often and ask for help, advice, and frank feedback.

3. Dedicate yourself to lifelong learning. Things move too fast to rely on what you learned in the past. To succeed in today's business world, you must be an avid student of business, strategy, technology, people, and culture.

4. Take everything you learn, and focus it on engaging your employees in serving the customer.

As I studied this incredible turnaround story, it reminded me a great deal of my work with IBM. In 1990, IBM was the second most profitable company in the world, with net income of $6 billion on revenues of $69 billion. In 1994, I was working as a consultant to the sales group of one of the major divisions of IBM. By this time the once great organization was standing at the precipice of bankruptcy: it had posted an $8.1 billion loss in the previous year, and its share price had dropped from forty-two dollars to just twelve dollars. To my mind, IBM suffered from three of the deadly habits that a seasoned bankruptcy lawyer once told me were the most common reasons for a company to fail:

Ignorance: It was not paying attention to the marketplace, not studying the competition closely enough, and not listening to their customers. It ignored the warning signs and turned inward toward turf guarding and politics rather than outward to the marketplace.

Indifference: An attitude of "we're Big Blue. Other companies might have to listen to the customer, but not us; we tell the customer what they should buy" was prevalent in every division I came into contact with. Years of blue suits, white shirts, and red ties made the IBM sales force feel as though they, not the customer, dictated the terms.

Inflexibility: Even when it became obvious that market share was slipping and the company was tumbling toward bankruptcy, the silos, hierarchy, and massive bureaucracy refused to budge. Divisions did not talk to each other, multiple salespeople called on the same account, and battles against other divisions of IBM to bring in business were being waged. When folks were called on the carpet about this self-destructive behavior, they made a few mea culpas and then went right back at it.

So what turned it around at IBM? The answer from Lou Gerstner, who, ironically, took over as the new CEO on April Fools' Day in 1993, is straightforward and clear: completely changing the culture toward transparency, teamwork, customer focus, and extremely fast action. From my study of the situation and personal experience working inside the company, it seems to me that the turnaround was based on four major strategies:

1. Create strong, collaborative partnerships with customers, and sustain an intense focus on the marketplace.

2. Drive unique value and growth through innovation and offering value-added solutions rather than products.

3. Invest heavily in finding, keeping, and developing the best people, and keep them focused on furthering our core competencies.

4. Leverage the skills and knowledge of those people through collaboration, communication, teamwork, and a strong sense of urgency.

How did this work for IBM? Between 1991 and 1993, IBM lost a breathtaking $16 billion. In what was termed the most remarkable turnaround of any company ever, IBM reported a net income of $7.58 billion on revenues of $89.13 billion ten years later, in 2003.

The ideas that Anne Mulcahy and Lou Gerstner used to turn around two of the largest companies on the face of the earth are not complex; they merely require focused effort and disciplined execution.

CHAPTER 5

Disciplined Execution

A PERFORMANCE-ORIENTED CULTURE THAT
DEMANDS FLAWLESS OPERATIONAL EXECUTION,
ENCOURAGES CONTINUOUS INNOVATION, AND
REFUSES TO TOLERATE MEDIOCRITY

There is a dynamic tension between this chapter and the previous one. I've just finished telling you that speed rules, a sense of urgency is critical, be fast or fail—and now I'm going to turn around and implore you to be methodical and disciplined in everything you do. Urgency *and* discipline: it seems like an oxymoron. But the two not only can coexist; they must. Speed, in and of itself, is useless without the will and determination of disciplined execution, the fifth of the six principles of business success. Otherwise you just continue to make the same mistakes, but even faster. The people in your organization need to have an overpowering desire to move quickly and get the important things done right now, married to a deep respect for the processes, systems, and tools that allow them to work at a fast pace and still deliver consistent excellent results. Straddling the line between speed, continuous innovation, and fast action taking on one side, and discipline, focus, and process on the other side, is a difficult balance to achieve, but great organizations do both.

How Bad Is It?

For several years, I have been a guest lecturer on strategic thinking and the fundamentals of strategic planning during a special leadership institute at the University of Pennsylvania's Wharton School of Business. Most years, between 100 and 130 senior executives attend my session, and I always ask the same question: "What percentage of the time do you feel organizations that have clear plans and goals and understand what they are trying to accomplish in the marketplace actually *execute those plans effectively?*" Year after year the answer has been the exact same: 10 to 15 percent.

That may sound far too pessimistic, but my experience working in hundreds of companies, large and small, has shown me that this number is accurate. You'll also remember that I mentioned lack of execution in Chapter One as one of the four key things that almost nine hundred senior executives I've presented to identified as a major roadblock to moving their businesses forward (along with poorly communicated vision, lack of courageous communication, and accepting mediocrity). The only thing more shocking than the low percentage of companies that effectively execute their plans is the staggering amount in lost revenues and waste that lack of disciplined execution costs those companies. Dozens of research studies indicate that failure to execute on major objectives can cost a business as much as 50 to

70 percent in lost revenues. I think the number is probably much, much higher, but either way, there is a good chance that a lack of effective execution is costing your organization a significant amount of wasted time, effort, resources, and, most important, money.

What we are talking about here gets to the crux of this book: it is one thing to understand intellectually what you need to do to make your organization successful, but a completely different thing to be able to create a culture of disciplined execution that takes great ideas and plans and turns them into consistently well-executed actions. Peter Drucker, the most famous management thinker of our time, identified the ability to deliver results as the primary skill of a leader and the only true measure of organizational effectiveness. Businesses that create sustained success are sharply focused on a set of core competencies and then relentlessly execute on those competencies better than the competition to create strategic advantage. Businesses that fail might have the best of intentions, good people, great products, and a solid plan for success, but they cannot deliver results because they are not disciplined in executing on their most important goals day in and day out.

Because lack of consistent execution is such a prevalent and incredibly costly problem, several of my clients asked me to build a class to address this issue.

The Nine Steps to Ensure Disciplined Execution

Although the title of this section specifies that there are nine steps to ensure disciplined execution, in fact none of the processes I put forward in this book are a paint-by-the-numbers remedy to everything that ails your business. Business improvement initiatives such as benchmarking, best-in-class studies, competitive intelligence, creative swiping, and all the others are essential tools in creating a great organization, but never think that you can simply pick up a process or strategy from another company and implement it in your company. You have to take the ideas in this book (or any other book) and figure out how they work best for your organization, your people, your customers, and your industry.

The six principles of business success, and the steps involved in implementing them, are *interdependent*. Vision is ineffective without communication, talent is ineffective without focus and systems, and systems are ineffective without speed and agility. This nine-step process (see Figure 5.1), by its very nature, encompasses all of the other things we have talked about to this point because it is a tool for ensuring that you can execute all six of the principles of business success effectively.

Step One: Vision and Values

The first step in creating an organization that is superb at disciplined execution is to set the context by clearly communicating (actually overcommunicating) the vision and the values of the organization and strongly emphasizing that only through the effective execution can the vision be attained. This step is important to help people remember why they are working so hard on the business and the way you expect them to act within the organization as they pursue aggressive goals on tight time lines. After all, execution is effective only if it supports the vision and is governed by the values.

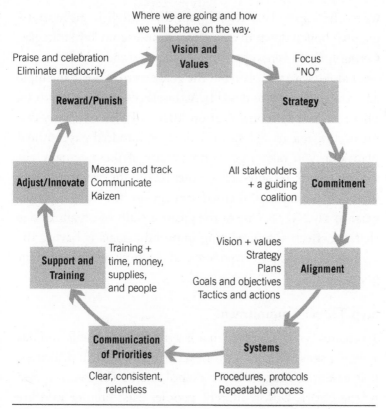

FIGURE 5.1 Nine Steps for Ensuring Disciplined Execution

Step Two: Strategy

One of the essential elements of creating a culture of disciplined execution is to keep the entire organization squarely focused on the handful of key strategies that drive the success of the business. It is extremely important to remember that not everything can be a priority. Organizations that are successful focus intensely on the few critical areas that will yield the highest possible return. I have worked with multibillion-dollar companies with offices spread across the globe that had their entire strategic plan boiled down to a single page and seven key strategies. Certainly there were supporting documents and other data that went along with the plan, but the goal was to make it as simple and straightforward as possible. At the other end of the spectrum, I have worked with organizations that had a list of twenty-two major strategic objectives in their three-hundred-page annual plan. Can you take a guess how many of these actually got implemented? To reiterate, another reason for creating a clear, intended outcome—a focused strategy—is also to tell people what to say NO to. One of the greatest skills of organizations that are effective at executing important goals is having the courage and discipline to not spend any time on unimportant goals.

Step Three: Commitment

To create an organization that is agile and adaptable and has a strong sense of urgency for executing on critical priorities, it is essential that all key stakeholders be fully committed to the effort. Unfortunately, people resist change and are often reluctant to be accountable for delivering ambitious results. The surest way I know to get people committed is to form a guiding coalition of the most respected and admired people in the company. If people across all areas of the business see that the top folks in the organization are excited, passionate, and personally committed to following through on the major objectives and being held accountable for their effective execution, they are much more likely to support the change. But if people see one or more of the key players in the organization resisting the change, bad-mouthing initiatives, and refusing to get on board, you can be sure there will be a mutiny. The guiding coalition must demonstrate 100 percent unity.

Step Four: Alignment

In this step you want to make sure that what you are trying to execute is in alignment with all of the other strategies, plans, goals, and actions of the organization. I have seen entire organizations implode when (typically through poor communications) departments were pitted against each other in an effort to execute mutually exclusive objectives. Fast decision making, agility, and effective execution require that all parts of the organization be completely aligned and moving toward the same goal. An excellent way to ensure alignment is to demand that all goals in the organization conform strictly to the SMART goal format. I am sure that most of you reading this book are familiar with the idea of SMART goals, but I've made a few subtle changes, so here is a quick review on how I approach SMART goal setting:

- *Specific.* Write precisely, and include plenty of detail so that it is easy to understand exactly what you are trying to achieve.

- *Measurable.* Goals must be quantifiable. You have to remove all ambiguity so there is no question as to whether you have accomplished the goal. The word I like to use here is *binary:* you either achieved it or you didn't; there is no middle ground. This is so important because it allows you to remove ego from the equation when discussing goal achievement. You never say,

"I don't feel that you achieved the goal," or "I don't think that's the right outcome." There is no opinion about it: the person either successfully reached the goal or didn't. In this way, you can be tough on numbers and details without being tough on people.

- *Agreed on.* In today's world of teamwork and collaboration, the achievement of any major goal typically involves multiple people, departments, and functions working interdependently. To be successful in that sort of environment, everyone must understand the goal and agree to participate in pursuing it.

- *Realistic.* Can the goal be achieved? Do you have the resources, time, people, money, skills, and knowledge to deliver this goal by the target date? Is it aligned with all of the other key goals of the organization? There are few things more demoralizing to a team than being assigned a goal that everyone knows is completely unrealistic. Setting stretch goals is one thing, but when the goals become ludicrous, they destroy morale and undermine respect for upper management.

- *Time-bound.* A goal without a firm due date and a specific owner is merely a wish.

Lots of organizations are great at generating cool ideas and developing impressive lists of "action steps," but until it is standard operating procedure that every action step is written as a SMART goal, given a hard due date, and assigned to a specific individual who will be held accountable for delivering it, there is little hope of creating a culture of disciplined execution.

Step Five: Systems

Would you want to fly with a pilot who didn't look at the pre-flight checklist? Have a surgeon operate on you who didn't bother to look at your chart? Allow a builder who never opened the blueprints to build your house? Absolutely not, and it is no different in your business. You don't want to roll out any important project in your organization unless it is underpinned with a solid and well-thought-out system to ensure repeatable success. The key words are "ensure repeatable success": the beauty of systems and process is that they allow consistent excellent performance.

Some organizations use total quality management, six sigma, or lean manufacturing; others use business process reengineering or advanced customer relationship management tools. I am not attached to any of these systems as long as you use something to make sure that your people have a clear, step-by-step process that allows them to consistently produce the desired positive results. When done properly though, systems and processes are not really about checklists; they are about establishing an organizational mind-set that is focused on consistently producing better and better results. Apple has a design process to ensure that every product it brings to market is both functional and elegant. Southwest Airlines has a gate turnaround process that allows it to load and unload planes faster than the competition, which equates to more time in the air making money and less time on the ground with frustrated passengers. Disney World has a robust guest service process to make sure that a visit to the park is magical.

Consistently superior results do not come from chance, fate, or good luck. They come from systems and processes that have identified all of the steps necessary to produce excellence and an organizational culture that embraces the concept of process as a competitive advantage. If you can consistently do things better, faster, and more efficiently while still delivering high-quality and superb service, you have developed a unique differentiator that is exceedingly hard for your competition to copy.

There is a warning here: establishing effective processes and systems within a large organization can be challenging and complex, far beyond the scope of this book. So be sure to take your time, ask for help seeking out the guidance of experienced people, and monitor the systems carefully to be confident they are delivering the specific results you desire.

Step Six: Communication of Priorities

Once you have established a focused strategy, gained the commitment of key stakeholders, ensured that goals are aligned with the rest of the organizational strategies, and created systems and protocols to deliver consistently successful results, you must relentlessly communicate to the entire organization why it is critical to stay the course and keep focused on executing the strategy. One of the biggest mistakes I see organizations make is to roll out a new program with loads of fireworks and fanfare, and then let it die on the vine a few weeks later. Any major change will take eight to eighteen months of continuous, relentless, consistent communication to keep it on track and moving toward success.

This is one of the most challenging parts of my job. When I take a senior management team away for a 2-day retreat, they expect the entire business to be changed within the next 10 days. When I tell them this will require a focused effort and massive communication for a minimum of 90 to 120 days until they start to see strong positive results, you can almost see the air go out of their tires. People think you have one meeting about something, show a few PowerPoint slides, and tell people you think it's important and everything will be fine from that point forward. Nothing could be further from the truth, which is that people have already forgotten the message in the PowerPoint before they walk out of the room. Clear, consistent, relentless communication of priorities is fundamental to creating a culture of disciplined execution.

Step Seven: Support and Training

People don't just stick a book under their pillow at night and wake up in the morning a genius on that subject. Learning by osmosis is a nice idea, but it doesn't work in the real world. People need lots of training and support to learn new skills and accomplish challenging tasks. I have seen multimillion-dollar initiatives completely fail because the organization did not invest the time, money, support, and training necessary to prepare people to succeed. They spent hundreds of thousands of dollars on the rollout, millions on the technology, and a measly $10,000 on a half-day training seminar. It's like building the space shuttle and not teaching the astronauts how to fly it.

It stands to reason that if people are your most valuable asset, you want that asset to be constantly appreciating. The only way to do that is to invest heavily in training and development, and make sure people have all of the tools, equipment, time, resources, and support they need to deliver the results you are asking for.

Step Eight: Adjust and Innovate

As my friends in the military are fond of saying, no plan survives the first shot fired. As soon as you begin to implement the initiative, things will start to go wrong, which is incredibly frustrating for the people who still believe that business is like a predictable machine. Business, especially today, is anything but predictable, and you need to be ready to adjust and adapt quickly to the steady stream of curveballs thrown your way. The first step in this process is to track the results your team is getting. Here are my thoughts on measurement:

- Measure only the very few key elements that truly drive success—not twenty to thirty things, just four or five key drivers.

- Just because something is easy to measure doesn't mean you should do it.

- Just because something is really difficult to measure doesn't mean you get to skip it.

- Once you identify the key measures that drive success, share the numbers with everybody.

- If the measurements are somewhat complex, teach everyone exactly what they mean.

- Make sure that rewards and compensation are tied directly to the key measures of success.

- Communicate the important measures, and where you stand on them, relentlessly.

Once you understand the key measures of success and have a system to track and communicate them, the next step

is to push the entire organization for continuous improvement around those key measures.

Perhaps the best-known tool for accomplishing this is
Toyota's world-famous philosophy of *kaizen,* or continuous
improvement. The idea behind *kaizen* is to instill in every
employee an insatiable curiosity to constantly look for ways to
do things better and reduce waste. What I like so much about
kaizen is that it does not require earth-shattering, completely
revolutionary, industry-changing innovation. Instead *kaizen*
means finding a way to make things just 1 percent better every
single day. If someone comes up with an amazing innovation
that totally changes the way you do business, fantastic; that's
great. But it does not take away the responsibility that every
single employee has of looking every single day at ways to
make things consistently 1 percent better. I love *kaizen* so much
because it does not seem daunting: I don't have to be a genius
or totally reinvent the way we do business. I just need to find
one little thing that I can do better in my job, every single day.

Step Nine: Reward and Punish

What gets measured and rewarded gets done. The number
one way to get people to effectively execute is to lavishly
reward those who do. And by *lavishly,* I do not necessarily
mean financially. I mean to be exceedingly generous with
praise, celebration, recognition, small rewards, and, yes,
sometimes very large rewards. From cruises to cash, from
days off to promotions, it is essential to have a robust rewards and celebration program to recognize people who execute to plan and deliver the required results in myriad ways.

Even more important is to create a culture that refuses to
tolerate mediocrity. Let me caution you here: I'm not saying

you just wipe out anybody who does not meet his or her goals. Far from it. One of my favorite Jack Welch quotes is, "I never fired anybody who was surprised." In other words, when someone starts to stumble and fall, you owe it to them to give them a hand, help them up, and try to get them back on track before you remove them from the team. The first step in dealing with a poorly performing employee is to go look in the mirror. Have you done everything in your power to support and help that person? Have you given clear direction? Does this person have all of the tools and equipment he or she needs? Have you given enough time and help to be successful? Have you communicated very clearly that his or her performance needs improvement? If you have done all of this and things are not getting better, then it is time for the three T's:

- *Train.* Send your employee to a seminar or training class, assign a mentor, pair him up with somebody who has the skills he lacks, give him some books, articles, CDs, DVDs. Do anything and everything you can think of to help him learn what he needs to know to be successful.

- *Transfer.* If the training doesn't work and he isn't learning the skills for his position, can you move him someplace else in the organization where he will be successful? I am not suggesting you shuffle him off to some other department and shift your problem on to someone else, but is there a place in the organization where this person will add real value and enjoy the work he does? It is a shame to lose a talented person because you moved him into a position he was not suited for. So before you dismiss him, look around to see where he might continue to contribute to the organization.

- *Terminate.* After you have exhausted all of the training, support, mentoring, and help you can possibly offer and determined that there is no place else in the organization where this person can successfully add value, then it is time to allow him to explore other opportunities. However, if you have really worked hard on the training, with lots of open and honest communication to the employee, it has been my experience that by this point, most people realize they just don't fit in the organization and are eager to go someplace else where they can succeed.

You must set high standards of performance for people across the organization and then be absolutely rigorous and hold them 100 percent accountable to meeting or exceeding the standards, without ever crossing the line and becoming ruthless in your pursuit of results. Years ago when I was a very young CEO and managing people as much as thirty years older than I, I had a hard time holding people accountable. It was difficult to tell someone twice my age that he was not living up to the standards I expected of him. One of the tools I developed to deal with this situation was what I called "the four-page performance review," which helped get the employee to hold himself or herself accountable instead of my having to do it. Here's how it worked.

When someone was not performing up to agreed-on standards and we had exhausted all of the normal management, training, and motivational tools, I would ask the person to take some time to fill out four specific pieces of paper.

On the first piece of paper, I asked him to write what he felt he could deliver to the organization over the next six months. I wanted it measurable and specific so there was no ambiguity at all about what the deliverables would be. I would ask him to be realistic but aggressive, understanding that we had an organization that did not tolerate coasting or mediocrity. He was in my office because of poor performance and needed to prove to me and everyone else that he could be a productive team member. Once he could, all would be forgiven and forgotten, but now, he needed to clearly show that he could add significant value to the business.

On the second piece of paper, I asked him to list everything (resources, training, support, and equipment) he needed from me and the rest of the organization to deliver what was on the first sheet.

On the third piece of paper, I asked him to write out what sort of rewards he wanted, within reason, if he delivered everything he promised.

On the fourth piece of paper, I asked him to write what the ramifications would be if he did not meet his goals after I gave him all of the support he requested. The vast majority of people listed termination.

After he completed these four lists, we would sit together in my office and after a little negotiation and clarification, we would both sign each of the pieces of paper and agree to hold one another accountable for delivering our promises. Then every week, I would have a fifteen- or twenty-minute meeting with that person to go over the four lists. We would sit down together, and I would say, "How are you doing on page number one? Is everything on track? Is there anything you need from me on the second piece of paper that I haven't delivered for you?" This is the main reason that I asked him to write the four pieces of paper himself, so there could be no confusion about exactly what they meant.

Some people were able to start to deliver the required results, but most people realized after only a few months that I had delivered everything on my piece of paper (support, training, resources, equipment) but they were not anywhere close to delivering what they had promised on their pieces of paper. At this point, they typically resigned. Using this method—the four pieces of paper written by the employee—I have had to fire very few people in my career, but I have had a number of low performers terminate themselves.

Effective execution is about everyone in the organization, at every level, holding each other mutually accountable for keeping their promises and delivering the results they have committed to. In a perfect world, you would not need a process to ensure that people kept their promises, but we all live in the real world where people need a tremendous amount of support, guidance, and systems to help them understand what the priorities are and how to execute them.

■ ■ ■

So there it is: years of work in the field, thousands of pages of reading, all boiled down to nine steps to ensure effective execution. I know they look simple, but think of a major project in your organization that is stalled or never got completed. Did you truly do every one of the nine steps effectively? When I ask that question in training sessions, the answer I usually get is, "No, we don't even get close to doing all nine of those steps." Great organizations set a clear vision for success, hire only the best people, foster a great culture with a free flow of information, create a sense of urgency, and then build the systems, processes, and procedures necessary to ensure effective, consistent, and disciplined execution.

SUMMARY OF KEY POINTS

- Urgency and discipline must coexist.
- Most organizations execute only 10 to 15 percent of their major goals.
- The four biggest roadblocks that almost nine hundred executives identified to moving their businesses forward are lack of a well-communicated vision, lack of courageous communication, lack of disciplined·execution, and tolerating mediocrity.
- Process and systems drive effective execution.
- There are nine steps for effective execution:
  1. Tie execution into the vision and values of the organization.
  2. Focus the organization on a few key strategies to execute.
  3. Put together a guiding coalition of key leaders who demonstrate personal commitment to being living examples of disciplined execution.
  4. Fully align all of the major strategies and objectives of the organization. Confusing priorities or those that are at odds lead to failure.
  5. Create systems and processes to ensure repeatable success.
  6. Once you have established a focused strategy and identified key priorities for execution, overcommunicate the goals and priorities to be sure that the entire organization is aligned and focused on the most important things.
  7. Give all of the training, support, resources, and help necessary to allow people to be successful in executing the key objectives.
  8. Expect the unexpected. Adjust and innovate continuously in response to the marketplace and the customer to ensure the organization is still focused on executing to the appropriate objectives.

9. Shower people who are effective in execution with praise, rewards, and recognition to demonstrate to the rest of the organization what behaviors are desired. Deal quickly and decisively with any person in the organization who is unwilling or unable to execute the key strategies.

- Use the three T's (train, transfer, or terminate) to deal with people who are unable to effectively execute the plan.

EFFECTIVENESS AUDIT

This brief audit will help you determine how well your organization is doing on the key items outlined in this chapter. It is essential that you be completely honest in scoring the questions. This is not an exercise to get the highest score; it is a diagnostic tool to discover areas that need focus and improvement. Score the following statements on a scale of 1 to 10, with 1 being strongly disagree and 10 being strongly agree.

1. Our organization is highly effective at executing all of our important initiatives._____

2. The key leaders in our organization set an example of disciplined execution. _____

3. Every major initiative within our organization has been translated into a SMART goal._____

4. Every major initiative in our organization has a firm due date and a clear owner who is 100 percent accountable for delivering the desired results. _____

5. There is a high level of mutual accountability throughout our organization for effectively executing on key initiatives. _____

6. Our organization has done an excellent job of ensuring that all major projects and initiatives are aligned. _____

7. We set realistic goals that everyone feels are aggressive but achievable. _____

8. We have superb systems and processes to ensure that we flawlessly execute on all important projects and initiatives._____

9. Our organization does a superior job of communicating the key strategies that everyone should be focused on throughout the organization._____

10. Our organization is highly flexible and able to adjust strategies to changes in the marketplace when necessary. _____

11. We have a culture that aggressively pursues continuous innovation. _____

12. We have a culture that strongly supports prudent risk taking and rewards employees for innovation and creativity. _____

13. We have a robust praise and celebration system that identifies the unique motivators of individual employees and rewards them appropriately for demonstrating superb execution._____

14. We have an organizational culture that refuses to tolerate mediocrity and deals decisively with anyone who does not clearly demonstrate disciplined execution and accountability. _____

EFFECTIVENESS AUDIT SCORING KEY
- A score of 9 or 10 indicates strength in your organization.

- A score of 7 or 8 is a good score but has room for improvement.

- A score of 5 or 6 is an area of concern. This score needs to be brought up because if it heads in the other direction, it could lead to serious issues.

- A score of 3 or 4 is in the danger zone and requires attention and resources to get it moving up the scale quickly.

- A score of 1 or 2 is an emergency and should be dealt with immediately.

THINGS TO THINK ABOUT
AND DISCUSS

It is important to take time and give the following questions some serious thought. Be honest with yourself, and think your answers through in detail. You might also find it valuable to gather several people from your organization to discuss these questions as a group, exploring how each of you might answer the same questions differently. These opposing points of view and alternative ideas are critical to developing quality answers.

1. What percentage of the time do you think your organization executes your major objectives effectively?

2. What are two or three key projects in your organization that were never successfully implemented?

3. What do you believe the impact has been to your organization because of an inability to execute on some of your major strategies?

4. Can you think of anyplace in your organization where strategies and priorities are not aligned? If so, what are they, and what has been the impact of this misalignment to the organization?

5. Could your organization give more training and support to enable people to be more effective at execution?

6. What are several innovative ways that you can reward employees who are excellent at delivering results?

7. What are several innovative ways you can foster more accountability throughout your culture in order to hold people accountable when they fail to execute effectively?

TURNING IDEAS INTO ACTION

Here are several suggestions on how you can take some of the main ideas of this chapter and begin to implement them immediately. Some of them might work perfectly for you; others will need some adjustment and customization. Read them carefully, and start thinking about how you can make them work in your organization.

1. Do a financial analysis of lost revenues and the opportunity cost that poor execution has on your business (for example, rework, missed deadlines, poor quality, lost customers, missed opportunities, holding up other departments). Post those numbers, and have a discussion throughout the organization about what the lack of disciplined execution is costing the entire business, and what everyone feels should be done about it.

2. Take the nine steps for ensuring disciplined execution outlined in this chapter, customize them to your organization, and begin using them at the start of every major initiative to ensure your team follows a step-by-step process for flawless operational execution.

3. Undertake a benchmarking project to measure the effectiveness of your organization against your key competitors and best-in-class to determine precisely where your organization needs to improve.

4. Hold a management meeting or off-site retreat to review all projects and initiatives and ensure they are fully aligned throughout the organization.

5. Create a guiding coalition of key people from across your organization to act as champions for disciplined execution and higher levels of accountability. Challenge these people to be a living example of the sort of behavior that you expect from your teams and encourage them to be cheerleaders for urgency with discipline.

CASE STUDY: CARL RAPP'S PHILOSOPHY OF BUSINESS EXCELLENCE

I have spent time crawling around in hundreds of companies across the globe and worked with thousands of executives, and there are none finer than Carl Rapp, the president and CEO of Philadelphia Gear Corporation (PGC makes state-of-the-art gearing solutions for power transmission applications worldwide). It is easy to tell when you meet Carl that he absolutely loves Philly Gear and all of the people who work there. I have had the great pleasure of working with Carl and his team for the past several years, and although he would be the first to point out that it is far from perfect, PGC is one of the best-run organizations I have ever encountered. When I asked Carl if I could interview him for this book he reluctantly agreed, insisting that the way they did business at Philly Gear was just "common sense, nothing particularly special or unique." Nevertheless, I think you'll see that Carl Rapp and his team have created something very special.

Raise Your Expectations

"Early in my career I worked for a company that set very low internal expectations. They felt we were in a mature industry, and the best we could do was just hold on to what we had, and that just seemed counterintuitive to me. That's when I learned not to compare yourself to your competition in your industry or even past performance; compare yourself to other great businesses or other great teams. You're going to achieve as much as you believe you can achieve. Whether you set the bar low or high, that's probably where you're going to end up."

Surround Yourself with Inspiring People

"My sense is if you get people who have—and this is my term— blue-collar upbringing with white-collar smarts, people who have learned from their family experience growing up the value of a buck, what hard work is about, what keeping promises means, I think you tend to get leaders who instill that in their individual teams. You want people who are hungry but intensely disciplined and intensely ethical. They all learned something at the knee of their dad or mom or grandmother who said to them, 'You don't get anything for free, and you're only as good as your word.' I like to be surrounded by people like that. It inspires me."

Run to the Problem

"When I got my first management position, I began to commit to paper the things I saw in upper management that impressed me and some of the things I thought were real problems. The one thing that really hit me early on was how absolutely excited management would be for new opportunities, yet how uninterested they were when things were going really bad with one of our customer relationships. This was the beginning of our 'Run to the Problem' mantra that we try to instill in everyone at PGC. At the end of the day, you should be willing to run as fast to problems as you do to an opportunity because that's more important to the customer or to the partner you are working with than how quickly you accepted a purchase order. It really speaks volumes to the character of your company that you're willing to go shoulder to shoulder with that customer or partner when things are not going so good, without laying blame and instead figuring out a way to solve their problem."

Be Honest with Yourself

"One of the things I'm the most proud of in our culture is the willingness for our management team to say, 'You know, we might have a lot of things going right, but this particular process or system doesn't work, and let's start there.' There are various tools you can use today to fix problems, whether it's *kaizen* or some of the lean tools, or a host of others, but it's first the willingness to say, 'We've got a problem.' In my position, you have to be able to boil down all of the problems of the company to the top two or three things at any one time and then relentlessly and ruthlessly address those top two or three. To create a great culture, you not only need to set your expectations high, you not only need to get people who understand the value of a buck and what it means to work really hard and keep promises, you not only need to run to problems, but you need to be honest with yourself so you can identify problems to begin with. Any company, any team, can only do a couple of things well at any one time. Focus on that stuff, get it done, tell people about it, and then move on to the next issue."

A Strong Sense of Urgency

"As the leader of an organization or team, you have to set a certain pace, and that pace has got to be built around listening and achieving important things, delivering a few substantive promises, and then moving on quickly to the next challenges. I've worked in organizations where they said, 'Everything we make is high quality,' or 'We don't need to be faster,' or 'Our customers will wait and we don't need to do anything about our costs,' and actually it was completely the opposite. You need to attack the issues that are important to customers, and your frontline people typically know what 90 percent of these issues are.

"I think this is another area where companies can benefit: you must regularly take the time to ask your customers how you are doing and then get it down to the top two or three issues that they are concerned about and then constantly work on resolving those issues. We use anonymous surveys and customer councils. You then have to articulate to your entire organization what the customer thinks is important, and that makes all the difference. Once you do that, it lets you focus your attention on building the tools for the people who have to work to serve the customer efficiently and effectively. It is staggering that a lot of companies talk about empowering people and giving their people the ability and freedom to make decisions, but they don't give them the tools. In any great company, you need good people, you need a strategy, you need common incentives, you need to communicate like crazy, and you need the tools that allow them to be successful."

People First

"In the old days, 80 percent of our life was spent fighting fires and 20 percent was on business that flowed through the company without any constraints. Today it's the reverse: 80 to 90 percent of what we do flows through, and we are fighting fires on the remaining 10 or 20 percent. I think the important thing to me is when we add a new SOP [standard operating procedure], we also look for what we can eliminate. In other words, we are constantly culling stuff out of the system that we no longer use—systems, processes, or reports. The reason is the focus issue.

"Everybody knows that there are processes required to put an order through the system. The goal of management should be to make that as painless as possible, with as many opportunities for taking out errors as possible. Yes, this saves time and money, but what you're really doing is eliminating waste so you can improve service to customers or other parts of the organization. The reason that systems and processes are so important is so that your people can be more effective and focused on the things that are truly value-added.

"This leads to the final point I'll offer. I've always struggled with this notion that people told me early in my career that the customer is everything: 'The customer should be your first and last thought of the day.' I've got to tell you that my first and last thought of the day is about the people inside my company because if I don't have the right people and treat them with a sense of urgency, professionalism, integrity, and look to make their work experience as efficient and positive as possible, how in the world can I turn around and ask them to treat my customers with a sense of urgency, integrity, professionalism, and efficiency? In a nonmonopoly business, the immutable law is that profit follows only quality and service; quality of service comes only from good people; and good people come and stay only where they are well treated."

CHAPTER 6

Extreme Customer Focus

OWNING THE VOICE OF THE CUSTOMER
AND CONSISTENTLY DELIVERING WHAT
CUSTOMERS TRULY VALUE

If I had a soapbox close by, I'd be on top of it. I believe so strongly that if you take everything else you have learned so far in this book—well-communicated vision for the future, best people, courageous communication and transparency, a culture of urgency, and disciplined execution—and focus all of it intensely on listening to your customers, delivering superior customer service, and building strong relationships with your customers, you will dominate your market. I said it earlier in the book, but it bears repeating: the only sustainable competitive differentiator left to most businesses today is creating a culture of continuous innovation and extreme customer focus driven by highly talented people. Competitors can copy your products, they can copy your processes and systems, they can buy or reverse-engineer your technology, and they can gain access to the same or similar distribution channels. In fact, they can meet or beat you on just about every front except for building a team of talented people who strive every day for continuous incremental improvements across the organization and deliver consistently superior customer service (as defined by the customer). It seems almost too simple to say that great customer service is a foundation of a truly great company, but it's the truth. And it is the final of the six principles of business success. And similar to the idea of hiring only the best people, almost every businessperson you talk to will enthusiastically agree that delivering excellent customer service is critically important. Yet almost nobody does it! Can you smell a huge opportunity?

Several years ago, I ordered an eighty-dollar book on business success, which even for me is a lot to pay for a book. When it arrived, I was dismayed to discover that it was only twenty-eight pages long, with big type and lots of pictures, which meant I paid roughly four dollars a page for this book. What's worse, in my opinion, was that the entire book boiled down to basically four key principles for business success:

- Show up on time.
- Keep your promises.
- Be extremely polite.
- Give a little bit more than is expected.

I felt I had been taken advantage of. But then I realized something amazing about that brief list. At the time, my wife and I owned two companies, were in the middle of building a custom home, and used to joke that we had an entire village of service people (pest control, lawn maintenance, car mechanic, computer guy, housekeeper) on the payroll.

I asked her to take a look at the four items and tell me if she could think of a single worker, vendor, subcontractor, or business we dealt with that consistently delivered those four things every time we interacted with them. The answer? No, not a single one. To prove this point, I ask you to take a minute or two and think about all of the suppliers, vendors, and businesses you deal with in the course of an average month. From strategic partners you deal with in your business, to your local dry cleaner, how many of them honestly deliver those four items to you every time you do business with them? Have I convinced you about the opportunity here yet?

Just in case you are still skeptical, let me throw a few numbers at you. I teach an intense class on how to deliver consistently superior customer service and did a huge amount of research to uncover the financial implications of improving customer service levels. I won't torment you with a bunch of statistics, graphs, and charts, but here is what all of the research shows: creating a culture of engaged employees who consistently deliver superior customer service can drive as much as an 85 to 104 percent increase in profitability. In other words, delivering great customer service can literally double your profit.

I have also conducted a number of surveys for my clients in which respondents said they would willingly pay a 15 to 25 percent price premium to buy the exact same product if they received truly outstanding service. In contrast, poor or inconsistent customer service is just about the surest way there is to chase customers away and doom your business to failure. Customers today demand to be treated extremely well and enjoy a wonderful purchasing experience. If you disappoint them in any way, they will simply go home and order a competitor's product off the Internet. Not only that, they might post an angry blog entry about your company and tell not just a few friends but every single person they know—and everyone beyond. If you Google "I hate . . . " you will have the choice of visiting Web sites dedicated to slamming Wal-Mart, the iPhone, Yahoo, Lotus Notes, Tom Cruise, Starbucks, Expedia, and many, many more. The upside to delivering consistently superior customer service is significant; the downside to not providing great service is devastating.

Although what constitutes superior customer service is somewhat unique to each individual customer, a broad array of national surveys demonstrates that these are the most important customer expectations for great service:

- *Reliability:* The ability to provide what was promised, on time, dependably, and accurately

- *Professionalism:* Highly knowledgeable, ethical, and honest employees who instill a sense of trust and confidence in the customer

- *Empathy:* Genuine care and concern for the complete satisfaction of the customer

- *Responsiveness:* Not just delivering prompt service but being proactive in anticipating the needs and concerns of the customer

- *Ambience:* The design and comfort of the physical facilities, cleanliness of the facilities and equipment, and appearance of the personnel

That list does not look particularly daunting, but ensuring that every single employee in your organization embodies it every single time they interact with a customer can be a monumental challenge. Although many factors go into building an organization that delivers fantastic customer service, I want to share with you what I believe are the four most important drivers of service excellence: attitude, moments of truth, voice of the customer, and employee engagement.

Attitude Is Everything

Several years ago, I attended a conference on customer service excellence where I worked with more than two hundred CEOs trying to uncover the essential elements of building a service-oriented culture. After a weekend of workshops, panel discussions, and breakout groups to combine the knowledge and experience of this extremely talented group of senior leaders, it was determined that the most important element in building the business that can deliver superb customer service is to hire for attitude and train for skills. It truly is just that awesomely simple. You can teach people to run a cash register, answer the phone, take an order, or work the sales floor, but there is not a training class on the face of the earth that can teach someone to have a positive and enthusiastic attitude about delivering outstanding customer service.

So the first and most important step is to find and hire people who are bright and talented *and* who love to serve other people and make them happy. If you can fill your organization with as many people like this as you can find, you are laying the foundation for creating a fantastic service culture in your organization. It is also important to realize that this is especially true for frontline service providers: housekeepers, cashiers, receptionists, delivery people, customer service operators, salespeople—anyone who has daily face-to-face interaction with your customers. A story should bring this into sharp focus.

I live in Florida, and the major grocery chain here is Publix. Whenever I give a talk about customer service to a group of people in Florida, I ask them, "How many of you personally know the family that owns the Publix supermarket chain?" I have never had anyone raise his or her hand to that question, so I go on to the next: "How many of you personally know the CEO of Publix?" Again, I have never had someone in one of my classes raise their hand in the affirmative, so I continue: "How many of you personally know the regional manager for your area?" Still no hands. "How many of you know the manager of your local Publix where you shop week-in and week-out?" At this point, I might see one person out of a crowd of several hundred raise a hand, so I move on to the last question: "How many of you know the cashiers and the baggers at your local Publix pretty well?" Nearly every hand in the room will go up.

Here's my point: the CEO and senior management team of Publix might be some of the nicest and most genuinely customer-focused people in all of humanity, but that is not how I judge the company. To me, the hourly-wage cashier who rings me up or the person who bags my groceries IS Publix Supermarkets. I will either continue to shop at Publix and give it my loyalty and my money, or I will take my business elsewhere, based in very large part on how well I'm treated by the cashiers and the baggers. Luckily, Publix does a pretty good job with its frontline folks, but it amazes me how many companies fail to realize that some of their lowest-paid and often least-respected employees are actually in the best position to make or break the future of the company. The more interaction an employee has directly with customers, the more essential it is to make sure this person has the tools, resources, training, and positive attitude to consistently deliver outstanding service. The companies that get it right, such as Starbucks, Ritz Carlton, Nordstrom, Disney World, and Southwest Airlines, enjoy not only a great reputation for consistently great customer service but also a dramatically stronger bottom line.

Moments of Truth

The process of delivering any product or service to a customer typically consists of multiple steps. Although every step is important, there are a few critical moments of truth that carry significantly more weight in the customer's mind.

Great service providers identify these critical touch points and are obsessive about creating systems and processes to ensure that they are delivered flawlessly every single time. For example, I made a list of every touch point I could think of in the process of a customer going out to dine at a restaurant. I won't give the complete list (I identified 157 touch points), but here are just a few to give you a flavor for what I'm talking about:

- Signage is clear, access to parking lot is convenient, and parking spots are wide enough for large cars and trucks.

- The parking lot is clean, landscaping is healthy and attractive, and the entrance is well lighted and safe.

- Immediately on entering, facilities are spotless, the ambience is warm and relaxing, and any music is at an appropriate level.

- The hostess greets patrons with a warm smile as they approach the reservations desk and welcomes them to the restaurant.

- The hostess offers to take jackets, determines the number of people in the party, and inquires to see if they have a reservation or a special seating request.

- The hostess determines the approximate wait for the table, informs guests of the time, and offers to bring beverages while they wait for their table.

- The beverage order is correct, and drinks are mixed appropriately and served in an attractive manner.

And those are just the first two minutes of a two-hour dining experience. As you can see, from pulling into the parking lot to driving away later in the evening after dinner, there are dozens of touch points that add up to either a positive or negative dining experience. However, out of all those various touch points, there are a few critical moments of truth that must go perfectly in order for the customer to be fully satisfied. For a restaurant, those critical touch points are:

- Cleanliness
- Food quality
- Service quality
- Price

You can be spectacular on all of the other touch points, but if you don't nail these four, there is no way to create loyal, highly satisfied customers. Consider what can happen:

- Really clean restaurant, pretty good food, okay service, outlandishly high prices = no game

- Superior food quality, very good service, reasonable price, cockroaches walking across the floor = out of business

- Very clean restaurant, highly attentive waiters, very reasonable price, poor-quality food = empty restaurant

The goal is to identify the short list of your company's key moments of truth—that is, your most critical customer touch points—and design processes and systems to ensure they are done absolutely flawlessly every time. The aim here is to make it as easy as possible for your people to provide stunning service by removing opportunities for mistakes or failures. Through checklists, standard operating procedures, computer systems, and regular training programs, you define exactly what superior customer service looks like in your business and then build a well-thought-out system to make sure that you can consistently deliver it.

Own the Voice of the Customer

Mark Twain once said, "The only critic whose opinion counts is the customer." It does not matter what you, or I, or your employees think is "great customer service." The only people who can make that determination are your customers, and the only way to find out what your customers want is to ask them, listen to them, and do everything you can to own their voice. Through surveys, customer panels, focus groups, help lines, expert users' groups, new users' groups, discussion boards, blogs, special events, trade shows, open houses, visiting customer locations, taking key customers to lunch, and a hundred more ways, it is essential that you spend the time, energy, and money necessary to find out as much as you can about the likes and dislikes of your customers and precisely how they define great customer service. How you go about collecting this information can be as complex or simple as you like. A school of thought in business right now says that asking a single question such as, "How likely are you to recommend our products and services to your family and friends?" can yield some valuable data. Some organizations do formal annual customer surveys, others ask customers to fill out a brief reply card at the time of purchase, and still others have extremely intensive customer relationship management systems that slice and dice customer data to determine even the most nuanced preferences. But the truth is that the great majority of businesses do absolutely nothing.

It is shocking to me how little most organizations know about the people who pay their bills, yet who is more important to your business than your customers? You can have stunning buildings, amazing products, and highly talented people, but if you don't have engaged and loyal customers, there is no way to sustain a successful business. It is very clear, at least to me, that the organizations that understand the customer better and then use that information to deliver superior service and build strong trusting relationships will enjoy the most success. Your challenge is to get as close as you possibly can to your customers in order to understand as deeply as possible exactly what will keep them engaged and loyal to your business.

Engagement Is the Engine

Highly engaged employees are the single greatest driver of customer satisfaction and loyalty, which is in turn the number one driver of organizational profitability and long-term success. This of course begs the question: What then drives employee engagement?

These are the factors that lead to strong employee engagement:

1. A vivid and compelling vision for the future of the organization *and* a clear customer service excellence vision that is meaningful and motivating

2. A culture of respect, encouragement, recognition, and praise

3. All of the training, tools, and resources necessary to perform their jobs superbly

4. A fair compensation system that is at least equal to what they would be paid to do a similar job at any other company

5. Setting high standards of performance and then holding people throughout the organization 100 percent accountable for meeting or exceeding the standards at all times

6. A culture of empowerment that supports prudent risk taking, innovation, and doing whatever it takes to deliver consistently superior customer service

If you can create an organizational culture that delivers these six factors to your employees in abundance, the likelihood is high that you will develop a group of highly engaged employees who will strive to deliver only the highest-quality products and services to your customers. To me, it is pretty straightforward: take great care of your people, and they will take great care of your customers.

SUMMARY OF KEY POINTS

- Great customer service is a foundation of building a truly great company.

- Take everything else you've learned in this book, and focus intensely on listening to the customer and delivering consistently superior customer service.

- Four key principles lead to business success: show up on time, keep your promises, be extremely polite, and give a little bit more than is expected.

- Superior customer service can drive as much as an 85 to 104 percent increase in your profitability.

- The most important customer expectations for great service are reliability, professionalism, empathy, responsiveness, and ambience.

- Hire for attitude; train for skills.

- Determine your organization's moments of truth, and ensure that those critical customer touch points are delivered flawlessly each and every time.

- Own the voice of the customer.

- Strong employee engagement leads to satisfied and engaged customers, which can lead to significantly higher profitability.

EFFECTIVENESS AUDIT

This brief audit will help you determine how well your organization is doing on the key items outlined in this chapter. It is essential that you be completely honest in scoring the questions. This is not an exercise to get the highest score; it is a diagnostic tool to discover areas that need focus and improvement. Score the following statements on a scale of 1 to 10, with 1 being strongly disagree and 10 being strongly agree.

1. Our leadership believes strongly that giving customers a consistently superior experience will lead to profitable growth. _____

2. Customer-focused employee behaviors are recognized and generously rewarded. _____

3. We have an engaging and inspiring customer service vision._____

4. Our entire business is organized around delivering consistently superior customer service. _____

5. We do an excellent job of owning the voice of the customer._____

6. Customer feedback is used to drive continuous improvement of our customer service delivery._____

7. We have a commitment to delivering high levels of customer service and refuse to tolerate anything less than superior customer service._____

8. In this organization, we set and enforce very high standards of performance. _____

9. We continuously measure customer satisfaction and engagement. _____

10. Maintaining very high levels of customer engagement and satisfaction is a top priority in our organization. _____

11. We have identified the critical few moments of truth that are essential to delivering consistently superior customer service in our business. _____

12. We have detailed and extremely thorough systems and processes to ensure a flawless delivery of our critical touch points each and every time we interact with the customer. _____

13. Our frontline customer-facing employees receive ample training, support, and resources to allow them to deliver superb customer service._____

EFFECTIVENESS AUDIT SCORING KEY

- A score of 9 or 10 indicates strength in your organization.

- A score of 7 or 8 is a good score but has room for improvement.

- A score of 5 or 6 is an area of concern. This score needs to be brought up because if it heads in the other direction it could lead to serious issues.

- A score of 3 or 4 is in the danger zone and requires attention and resources to get it moving up the scale quickly.

- A score of 1 or 2 is an emergency and should be dealt with immediately.

THINGS TO THINK ABOUT AND DISCUSS

It is important to take time and give the following questions some serious thought. Be honest with yourself, and think your answers through in detail. You might also find it valuable to gather several people from your organization to discuss these questions as a group, exploring how each of you might answer the same questions differently. These opposing points of view and alternative ideas are critical to developing quality answers.

1. Looking at your competitors, where does the level of customer service you deliver rank in comparison to what they offer?

2. What do you believe are the top three to five moments of truth in your customer service delivery chain?

3. What are five new and innovative ways you could improve the level of service you deliver immediately?

4. What are five new and innovative ways your organization can make sure it is hiring people with a positive, service-oriented, can-do attitude?

5. What are the top three companies you admire most for their ability to deliver superior customer service? What is it about these companies that makes their customer service so spectacular?

6. What would have to change inside your organization for you to create a culture of extreme customer focus?

TURNING IDEAS INTO ACTION

Here are several suggestions on how you can take some of the main ideas of this chapter and begin to implement them immediately. Some of them might work perfectly for you; others will need some adjustment and customization. Read them carefully and start thinking about how you can make them work in your organization.

Here is a short list for creating a culture of extreme customer focus:

1. **Create a customer service vision.** Much like creating a vision statement to direct the organization, also create a clear and compelling customer service vision that describes the level of service your organization aspires to deliver.

2. **Infuse your entire organization with the voice of the customer.** Create strong, trusting relationships with your customers. Solicit feedback, communicate that feedback throughout the entire organization, and then be sure to take action on the feedback your customers have given you.

3. **Become an expert on delivering superior customer service.** Find out everything you can about how to deliver great customer service. Steal the best ideas, benchmark against the top performers, share that information across your organization, and make learning about and working on improving customer service a core competency of your company.

4. **Turn every employee into a customer service champion.** Make serving the customer (both external and internal customers) the number one job of every employee in your organization. Help them with the tools, training, equipment, and support they must have to deliver excellent service consistently. Reward and praise those who deliver above and beyond the call of duty, and deal quickly and effectively with any employee who does not embrace the service values.

5. **Destroy any barrier that stands in the way of delivering superior service to the customer.** Look at all systems, policies, procedures, reports, and rules. Wipe out anything that creates roadblocks or frustrations in the effort to delight and amaze the customer. Stupid rules that make it hard for employees to serve superbly can kill your business.

6. **Measure, measure, measure, and communicate.** Create a clear, specific and extremely well-thought-out and overcommunicated program for systematically collecting and quickly communicating the most important customer service delivery measurements to the people who can then act on them. Make it easy for your people to win.

7. **Walk the talk.** Every level of the organization, starting at the very top, must be a living example of your service strategy. If the senior managers in your organization do not deliver excellent service to their internal customers by promptly returning phone calls, showing up on time for meetings, being well prepared, and acting professionally, there is absolutely no hope that your frontline people will deliver great service. All employees must demonstrate an obsession for delivering consistently superior customer service inside and outside the company.

CASE STUDY: CUSTOMER SERVICE EXCELLENCE THE AUSTIN OUTDOOR WAY

A few years ago, I had the incredible good fortune to get hired by Austin Outdoor to do some leadership training and strategy work with its management team. Austin Outdoor is one of the nation's premier professional landscaping operations that creates, builds, and maintains very high-quality landscaping projects for some of the top resorts and residential developments in the southeastern United States and Bahamas.

From the moment I met executive vice president Bill Dellecker and the other members of his management team, I was deeply impressed. The entire organization exudes professionalism, passion for the client, respect for employees, and unbridled enthusiasm that I have seen in very few other businesses. I am often called to help companies that are struggling, so it has been a real pleasure to work with an organization that has so many things going right. Yet even with things going so well for Austin Outdoor, it is constantly looking for ways to make the organization even better. It was this passion for continuous improvement that prompted Bill to ask me to work on the quality of customer service his folks delivered. For this case study, I asked Bill to outline how the customer service excellence (CSE) initiative has unfolded in his organization and what sort of impact it has had on his employees and customers.

A Shift in Focus

"The theme that we have recently established to focus our management team is 'Success by Design.' We've rallied around this idea because we believe that success by design is achieved through a series of integrated activities, consciously performed and then continuously refined. This represented a shift in our thinking from the focus we had previously promoted, which was 'sharpen your edge' to get better in each component of the

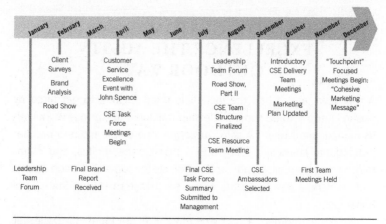

January	February	March	April	May	June	July	August	September	October	November	December
Client Surveys Brand Analysis Road Show		Customer Service Excellence Event with John Spence CSE Task Force Meetings Begin					Leadership Team Forum Road Show, Part II CSE Team Structure Finalized CSE Resource Team Meeting		Introductory CSE Delivery Team Meetings Marketing Plan Updated		"Touchpoint" Focused Meetings Begin: "Cohesive Marketing Message"

Leadership Team Forum | Final Brand Report Received | | | Final CSE Task Force Summary Submitted to Management | | CSE Ambassadors Selected | First Team Meetings Held

FIGURE 6.1   Customer Service Excellence Timeline

business, such as deploying new financial systems, deploying new field training and quality control systems—really working on individual pieces, individual departments, and individual districts to get better at the things we needed to do more effectively. This is especially important because we had experienced more than 500 percent growth over the past five years. The rate of growth had really outstripped our systems and people and a lot of other things, but what came to the forefront as we moved our company to the next level was the idea that we have some good systems and improved capabilities, but we really needed to shift the focus from those individual elements to creating a system where they all worked flawlessly together . . . integrated systems, consciously performed and continuously refined."

Involves the Entire Organization

"As we rolled out these concepts with our leadership team [Figure 6.1] we talked about where we've been as a company, where we're headed, and what it's going to take to get there. For the first time in our company, we began a series of road show events to share this shift in focus and these ideas with our various district locations. That was a transforming event because it really revealed the unique things that were happening at a local level and prompted some much deeper thinking. The ideas that we shared with all of our Austin team members were ones that we had been working on over the last couple of years:

1. Teamwork is mandatory, not optional.

2. We must be passionately focused on driving our clients' success.

3. Customers must always be the first beneficiaries of any changes we make.

4. Act in a boundary-less fashion, always looking for and applying the very best ideas regardless of origin.

"As I was riding back in the car from the last of the road show presentations with our VP of business development, we realized (one of the light-bulb moments for us) that we needed to focus on our frontline service delivery personnel in just the same way we focused on quality controls, our financial systems, and all the other parts of the business. We hadn't, in a systematic way, pulled them together and worked on the tools and systems of customer service excellence in the same way we had in other parts of the business, and if we really wanted to achieve this integration and improvement, that was one of the areas we needed to focus on."

Ask and Listen

"That prompted a much more intense look at our customer service excellence process, which led us to reach out to our clients and ask them to tell us what was important to them. We invited a panel of key decision makers from five of our biggest clients and asked them to speak frankly to us on what they loved about our company and the service we delivered, what frustrated them, and what we needed to do to fix those issues and keep them extremely satisfied and loyal. As a company, this was the first time we had ever pulled together all of our first-line managers and our frontline service delivery personnel who touch the clients on a daily basis in this sort of a format . . . directly interacting with the group of our top clients. It was revolutionary. Our people were on the edge of their seats listening to what our clients had to say, and what they had to say was powerful. They told us exactly what was important to them, exactly what they wanted, and exactly what the things were that bothered them. They gave us incredibly powerful feedback and everyone there was inspired by it.

The challenge was what to do with that information, how to discipline ourselves to really understand what they told us and then turn it into something that was actionable, and repeatable, and teachable so that we could carry it out throughout the entire organization. And on the client side, amazingly enough, they told us it was the first time a supplier had ever asked them to participate in something like that, so they were more than willing to open up and tell us exactly what was on their minds. It was a huge win for both sides. So that focus on our frontline personnel and what it was going to take for them to carry out their customer service mission day in and day out really crystallized at that point."

Create Clear Alignment

"The next phase was much more complicated. Once we had all of that raw information from our clients, the challenge was figuring out what we needed to do to turn it into actionable ideas and embed it into the culture of our organization. This led to the development of our Customer Service Excellence (CSE) task force. The CSE task force was composed of representatives from each of our various locations who worked together in a series of workshops over the next couple of months to frame what they'd learned into some concepts for moving the business forward. The concepts that we now refer to as the 'AUSTIN Absolutes' had emerged from the task force and gave us a way to translate our core values and beliefs into specific principles for action. [See Figure 6.2.]

As we looked at the **AUSTIN** Absolutes — **A**ttitude; **U**nderstand our clients; **S**urpass all expectations; **T**rust; **I**nitiative; and **N**ever be satisfied—and saw that they all build cumulatively on one another, we had another light-bulb moment. We suddenly

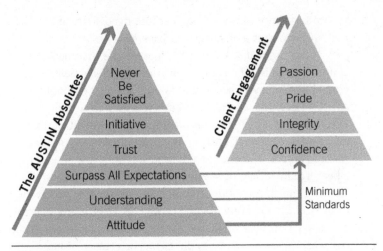

FIGURE 6.2 The AUSTIN Absolutes

realized that the way those principles build on one another aligns directly with the principles of client engagement developed by the Gallup organization through their Human Sigma concept. We adapted our culture accordingly, with the goals of building the client's confidence in Austin Outdoor, always behaving with complete integrity, resulting in their feeling of pride for the relationship we build with them, and ultimately building true passion as a result of Austin Outdoor's focus on the client's success."

A Never-Ending Process

"We then realized that if we wanted to translate these principles into action, we needed a system to do that effectively, and what emerged from that was a completely restructured two-tier customer service excellence approach. On the first tier is a central Customer Service Excellence Resource Team, which focuses only on the things that the local offices cannot handle independently: the information, the resources, or the training that is needed to overcome a challenge at the local level, something they could not reasonably do for themselves. The second tier is a local Customer

Service Excellence Delivery Team, because the delivery of customer service is a uniquely local experience.

"What we realized during this journey was that the Austin Outdoor brand is not a static thing; it is either being built up or eroded through every action that takes place on the front lines at a local level. We also recognized that delivering customer service excellence is a continuous process and not something that we could do instantaneously or as a one-off event. We needed to focus on one element at a time and work our way around the wheel, systematically, over a period of time, and believe that if we put as much conscious effort and focus onto each and every element, each and every month . . . we knew that over a year to eighteen months we would see a measurable improvement in our customer service and the way our clients perceive us in the marketplace.

"Striving for customer service excellence is a system that we have now hardwired into the organization as a way of thinking and being, the same way we have hardwired in financial systems, quality control systems, safety systems—so that everyone understands that providing exceptional customer service is not accidental; it is a conscious and repeatable process. But to be effective, the essence of this needed to be something that was meaningful to each and every employee, each and every stakeholder in Austin Outdoor. So we continue focusing everyone's attention on what we've referred to as our 'Wildly Important Goal' of 'Creating Premier Properties. Building Lasting Relationships.' At its core, it's as simple and as complicated as that. It's a given that we have to be able to deliver quality products and service; that's the price of admission, the 'Creating Premier Properties' part. However, 'Building Lasting Relationships' is the piece we added in order to enable the company to grow and have sustainable success over time."

CONCLUSION

What Do You Do Now?

We have covered a lot of ground together, but your journey has just begun. As I said earlier, it is one thing to read a book, and something completely different to take what you've learned and turn it into positive results. As you look back over the pages you've just read, keep in mind:

- The need for a well-communicated vision of the future of your organization.

- The understanding that finding and hiring the best people is critical to business success.

- The realization that honesty, transparency, and respectful candor are a cornerstone of building a solid communications structure throughout your organization.

- The importance of creating a culture of urgency that is focused on getting the most important things done quickly, combined with a high level of discipline to ensure flawless operational execution.

- That extreme customer focus is mandatory if you expect your organization to survive and thrive in the future.

In other words, these are the keys to business success. Hire bright, talented people who have a positive, service-oriented attitude. Communicate openly and honestly with them, sharing as much information as possible, and work especially hard to overcommunicate a vivid, clear, compelling vision of an ennobling and meaningful future of the company and your key business strategies. Give them all of the training, resources, and support they need to do their jobs efficiently, effectively, and quickly, while creating the systems and processes to make it easy for them to consistently deliver the standard of excellence required. Then take all of those elements, and focus them with great intensity on the voice of the customer in order to meet and exceed the precise needs, wants, and desires of the people you serve.

When it is all right in front of you like that, it is pretty easy to see the interdependence and synergy among the six principles of business success, each building on the next, all the various elements working together to create a highly successful enterprise. However, I don't want you to feel overwhelmed and think that you have to go out and address all six principles right now. (Remember *kaizen:* 1 percent better every day.) The goal is to figure out where you can create the most leverage immediately—the two or three places that will have the biggest positive impact—and begin with them. Here are some ideas to help you get started:

1. Go back through the entire book, and put a star or circle around any of your scores on the audits that scored 5 or lower. Is there a pattern? Do they all seem to revolve around a few critical areas in which your organization needs to improve?

2. Now go back and read all of the questions in the various chapters to see if your answers have changed in any way.

3. Take a look at the "Turn Your Ideas into Action" sections, and identify the top five action steps you believe are the highest priority. Rewrite them as they relate specifically to your business. For each of them, create a short list of SMART goals that you can begin to implement in the next thirty days.

4. Create a task force or small team that goes through the entire book together, comparing and contrasting scores on the various audits, discussing the questions in each chapter, and working together to identify the most important action steps to be taken immediately.

5. Ask the task force or team to make a presentation to the top managers, to gain their approval and support for implementing their most useful suggestions.

6. Go to www.awesomelysimple.com for additional resources, tools, audits, questions, worksheets, and information to help you better understand and implement all of the ideas in this book. There you'll also find discussion boards where you will be able to build a network of people to help you and then share your success stories and help others take action on the ideas in this book.

7. Identify three new people you can bring into your network of mentors and advisors. Gain their agreement to assist you, and get in the habit of asking them for help and advice often.

8. Identify three people you can act as a mentor to. It is surprising what you can learn when you are asked to

teach. In addition, this is another wonderful way to increase your network.

9. Take three of the tools listed in this book, such as four-level decision making or the four-page performance reviews, and begin using them immediately.

10. Create an internal survey to assess how well your organization is performing on the six principles. Use the feedback from your employees to design training programs and initiatives for immediate improvement.

11. Create a brief customer satisfaction survey, and send it to as many of your customers as possible. Use the feedback from this survey to improve service delivery and increase customer engagement and loyalty.

12. Identify your top stakeholders (key customers, shareholders, partners, vendors, key employees), and start asking one of them to lunch every week to discuss how they feel your organization is performing on the six principles.

13. Undertake a serious benchmarking initiative to directly compare your performance on key measures against the best in your industry—and the best in the world.

14. Ensure that you have developed extremely clear standards of performance, and communicate them like crazy. Then hold people 100 percent accountable for meeting or exceeding the standards at all times.

15. Begin tracking all of your major initiatives, and clearly post the results so that everyone in your organization can understand how well you are executing on the most important issues.

16. Set a realistic time line for implementing these changes—eight to eighteen months of extremely focused and disciplined effort—before you start to see any significant and lasting change.

17. Build the six principles of business success into your culture. Discuss these principles with potential employees, and get their commitment to follow the six principles before they are hired.

18. Look for and share success stories with your team. Catch people doing things right, and tell everyone about it. Pass along positive customer feedback. Show your folks how they can clearly link the effective implementation of the six principles of business success directly to your company's increased business success.

19. Above all else, make sure at the end of the day that everyone in your organization is having fun.

Final Thoughts

Several years ago one of my clients asked me to put together a special presentation for sixteen hundred people in their organization on what I felt were the fundamental drivers of achieving excellence in business and life. And my time slot to deliver this life-altering message was a mere fifteen minutes. To add insult to injury, the CEO of the organization indicated to me that only a roaring standing ovation would be acceptable at the end of my presentation. Let's just say I felt a little pressure.

For more than two months, I scoured my personal library and called the presidents and CEOs of every company and college I had ever had as a client in search of the answer. I won't drag you through the entire painful process, but in the end I was able to boil down all of the information I gathered and all of the advice I received into what I call the three watchwords of excellence.

The first watchword is *focus*. To achieve excellence in any endeavor in your life, you must first create a clear vision of what excellence truly looks like to you, then focus intensely on that picture every single day. I like to call this your philosophy of excellence: a vivid vision of what you hope to accomplish, the legacy you want to leave, the impact you want to make on the world as a result of striving for excellence.

The second watchword is *discipline*. Once you have determined your philosophy of excellence, you must have the discipline to take the steps necessary to achieve it. You do this by asking some important questions: Whom do I need to get on my team to achieve my vision? What new skills must I obtain in order to be able to reach the level of excellence I desire? What kind of knowledge or information will I need? How can I find these people and learn this information? Where do I need to go to locate these people and get the information? To achieve any level of excellence, you must be constantly curious about what you must do to reach the next level, and then have the discipline to do it.

The third watchword is *action*. The amount of excellence you achieve is directly proportional to the amount of focused and disciplined action you apply to your journey. A little bit of effort will deliver only minimal results. Massive action that is focused and disciplined can yield truly incredible results.

So the three key watchwords of excellence are *focus, discipline,* and *action.* If you are missing any of these, the outcome will most certainly be mediocre. And once you start accepting mediocrity, you become a magnet for mediocrity.

One of my favorite sayings of all time is that successful people willingly do what unsuccessful people are unwilling to do. My final question to you is this: Are you willing to apply the focus, discipline, and action necessary to use the information in this book to make your organization truly excellent? My great hope is that you are.

ACKNOWLEDGMENTS

Special thanks to my incredible literary agent, Giles Andersen; the immensely talented editor Erin Moore; and especially Karen Murphy and the entire team at Jossey-Bass for their hard work, professionalism, and tremendous faith in this project.

My true gratitude and friendship to Bill Davidson, Bill Dellecker, Tony DiFranco, Doug Hopkins, Song Kim, Hirofumi Leung, Jack Malcolm, Carl Rapp, Carolyne Salt, Roger Strickland, and of course, my valued clients. Without all of you, this book would not exist.

ABOUT THE AUTHOR

John Spence has earned a reputation as a leading authority in the areas of strategic thinking and planning, high-performance teams, advanced leadership development, and delivering consistently superior customer service. He is one of the most highly sought after executive educators and professional speakers in America.

For the past fifteen years, Spence has traveled upward of two hundred days a year presenting employee training workshops, keynote speeches, and executive coaching to more than three hundred organizations worldwide, including Microsoft, IBM, GE Capital, Genentech, Abbott Labs, Black Rock, the U.S. Navy, the Mayo Clinic, Alltel, Verizon, Qualcomm, State Farm Insurance, and dozens of private companies, associations, government offices, and nonprofits. He has also been a guest lecturer at over ninety colleges and universities across the United States, including Cornell, Rutgers, Brown, Stanford, and the Wharton School of Business at the University of Pennsylvania.

Spence has served as "executive in residence" for the University of Central Florida's Technology Incubator; as a special advisor to the Rawls College of Business at Texas Tech University; as a lead instructor for the University of North Florida's executive education division; on the board of directors for the University of Florida's Center for Entrepreneurship and Innovation; as an advisor to the University of Florida Leadership Development Institute; and as a senior instructor at the Cornell University Leadership Development School.

INDEX

A

Abbott Labs, 27, 53

Action, 182. *See also* Implementation of new ideas

Alignment, 135–136

Alltel, 53

Ambience, 158

Apple, 137

Approachability, 55

Attitude: Austin Outdoor's absolutes of, 174; for excellence in customer service, 159–161; for successful communication, 97

Audits: on communication, 91–93; on customer service, 167–168; on execution, 147–148; how to use, 13, 14; on sense of urgency, 122–123; on talent, 58–59; on vision, 28–29

Austin Outdoor, 171–176

B

Body language, 72–73

Buffett, Warren, 126

Bureaucracy, 107–109

Business leaders. *See* Leaders

Business success: basic requirements for, 11–12; customer service–related practices for, 156–157; importance of speed for, 101–102; interdependence of principles of, 129–130, 132, 178; measurement of, for disciplined execution, 140–141; principles of, 2–3, 177–178; simplicity of, 2, 3–4

communications, 67–71; importance of atmosphere issues in, 49–53; statement of, 33; that supports talent, 63–64

Culture of urgency. *See* Sense of urgency

Customer service, 10–11, 155–176; attitude's role in, 159–161; audit on, 167–168; creating culture focused on, 169–170; customer expectations of, 158; employee engagement needed for, 165–166; example of company with excellence in, 171–176; financial implications of improving, 157; gathering information from customers for, 163–165; importance of quality of, 155–158; key points on, 166; moments of truth (touchpoints) in, 161–163; questions for discussing, 168–169

D

Davidson, Bill, 61–64

Decision making: change of direction needed in, 106–107; clear, intended outcome necessary for, 103–106; by groups, 111, 112–117; levels of, 110–112

Dellecker, Bill, 171–176

DiFranco, Tony, 43–44

Direction, clarity of, 103–107

Discipline, 182. *See also* Execution, disciplined

Disney World, 137, 161

Dragonfly Sushi & Sake Company, 33

Drucker, Peter, 131

E

Emotions: communication focused on, 76; "the gap" technique for controlling, 87–89

Empathy: for customer service, 158; for organizational communication, 67

Employees: attitude of, 159–161; compensation system revised by, 69–71; engagement by, 165–166; intolerance of mediocre performance by, 141–145; organizational

Implementation of new ideas: about communication, 94–95; about customer service, 169–170; about execution, 149–150; about sense of urgency, 124–125; about talent, 60–61; about vision, 30–31; suggestions for beginning, 178–181

Improvement efforts, 140–141

In Search of Excellence (Peters and Waterman), 6, 12

Intel, 107

Intellectual rigor, 68

Interpersonal communication, 71–78; audit on, 92–93; body language's role in, 72–73; "hot words" in, 76–78; importance of skills in, 71–72; levels of listening in, 73–74; logical vs. emotional focus in, 76; sensory modes' influence on, 74–76

I-statements, 79–81

K

Kaizen philosophy, 141, 178

Kawasaki, Guy, 20–21

L

Leaders: characteristics of, demanded by top talent, 53–57; communication of vision by, 35–36; demands on time of, 1–2, 7–8; issues of concern for, 24–26; negatively affecting corporate culture, 49–53; organizational communications as viewed by, 66–67

Learning styles, 74–76

Listening: empathetic, as stage of conflict, 79; how to improve skill in, 74; levels of, 73

Logic, communication focused on, 76

M

Malcolm, Jack, 95–99

Managers. *See* Leaders

Mayo Clinic, 46

Meaning, and talent, 46

Measurement, 140–141, 170

Mediocrity: consequences of accepting, 183; as concern of leaders, 25–26; personnel policies to eliminate, 141–145

Strategy, focused, 133–134
Success. *See* Business success
Systems and processes,
137–138

T

Talent, 9, 37–64; audit on,
58–59; characteristics
of leaders demanded by,
53–57; characteristics
of top, 38–40; corporate
culture attracting and
supporting, 45–53,
63–64; for disciplined
execution, 151; finding and
recruiting, 40–44, 62–63;
implementing new ideas
about, 60–61; importance
of management of, 37–38,
44–45; interview with
successful leader on, 61–64;
key points on, 57; network
of, for sense of urgency,
119–121; questions for
discussing, 59–60. *See also*
Employees

Teams: decision making by,
111, 112–117; and great
leaders, 55–56; how to use
book with, 13–14

Ten-year rule, 4

Terminating employees,
141–145

Touchpoints in customer
service, 161–163

Toyota, *kaizen* philosophy of,
141, 178

Training, 139, 142

Transparency, 68–69

Twain, Mark, 163

U

Urgency. *See* Sense of
urgency

V

Values, corporate, 22–24. *See
also* Vision

Values statements: defined,
18, 19; examples of, 19, 33;
how to create, 19–20

Vision, 8–9, 17–36; audit on,
28–29; benefit of, 21–22;
communicating, 25, 26–28,
34–36, 105, 132, 178; and
corporate values, 22–24;
creating statement of,
19–21; implementing
new ideas about, 30–31;
importance of, to fast
decision making, 105; key
points on, 28; questions

for discussing, 29–30; terminology associated with, 17–19

Vision statements: defined, 18, 19; examples of, 19, 32, 33; how to create, 19–21

W

Waterman, Robert, 6, 12

Web site, for further information, 12–13, 179

Welch, Jack, 24, 142

WorldCom, 23

X

Xerox, 125–126